One
Fine
Day

SAMEER BHIDE

One Fine Day

Overcoming Adversity and Embracing
the New Normal with Grace and Gratitude

 PUBLISHING

DISCLAIMERS

The author is not providing any medical or professional advice in this memoir. The author does not prescribe the use of any technique or practices as a form of treatment for any physical, emotional, or medical problems without the advice of a physician or a professional, directly or indirectly. The author's intent is only to provide information of a general nature based on his experiences to help you in your quest for physical, emotional, and spiritual well-being. In the event you use any of the information in this book, the author and publisher assume no responsibility for your actions.

Cataloging-in-Publication Data is on file with the Library of Congress

Paperback ISBN: 978-1-7356934-4-6
eBook ISBN: 978-1-7356934-6-0

Interior design by K. M. Weber, ilibribookdesign.com

Printed in the United States of America

To my late father,
my late grandmother, and
my two amazing brave
sons, Jai and Arjun

Contents

Foreword

In his book, *One Fine Day*, Sameer Bhide sends each of us a reminder about the preciousness of life. Too often, as he points out, we take our lives for granted or, even worse, allow our setbacks to define us. Instead, he encourages us to take inventory of our blessings, to prepare to live a resilient life, and to be everlastingly grateful. What a wonderful way to live: blessed, ready, and grateful.

Imagine suffering a catastrophic stroke and brain hemorrhage leading to an induced coma and years of extraordinarily difficult recovery. Add to that, marital strains caused by the aftermath of the event led to divorce. This would be enough for anyone to spiral into deep depression and to second guess the value of life. Not so for Sameer. In his own words, he chose to overcome and embrace his new life with "grace and gratitude."

Recalling sometimes incomplete or distorted memories, *One Fine Day* recounts Sameer's simple and complete life just before his health crisis and weaves its way through traditional and atypical recovery treatments over many years. Along the way, Sameer shares with us his discoveries, reflections, and revelations accumulated from an unrelenting will to recover and live his best new life. This embodies the truest spirit of resiliency. Particularly interesting are the wide array of treatments used to heal, ranging from well-accepted scientific protocols to existential remedies. Highlighted are the love and humanity expressed by his caregivers. There are also occasional flashbacks to his childhood in India, travel logs, and health reports, which serve as interesting tidbits.

For unawake working professionals, or others who fail to recognize the joy of our daily mundane lives, the events leading up to the near-death disaster are eerily like what I see many of us do every day: catch up on emails, make a few calls, or manage workloads. This adds to the shock factor when Sameer is struck by proverbial lightning. This drives part of the message home, as our inability to see blessings in the present moment allows apathy to steal the quality of our lives away. Sameer is constant on this: we all must be prepared for life-changing moments, good or bad.

Interestingly, the most dominant theme in the book is gratefulness. I found the concept to be strange, coming from someone whom I perceive has lost so much. However, Sameer masterfully describes his gratefulness for a childhood he remembers with such joy and wonder; for a family that brought him love and purpose; and for the doctors, nurses, and practitioners who helped to heal him. Most importantly, he expresses his gratefulness for being alive to continue to learn, teach, and care for the well-being of others.

Pleasantly, Sameer shares personal lessons taken from adversity, humility, and resolve. Think of these as flowers in a garden, waiting to be enjoyed as they bloom at the end of each chapter. I found these learnings to be relevant to me and to be reminders about what is truly important about life. I am certain that you, too, will better understand how to live your better life guided by Sameer's principles that tell us every day is preparation for your life tomorrow. You only discover your life's purpose when you realize that you have no control, and surrender, and that happiness arrives at the harmonious intersection of your body, mind, and soul through the wonders of humanity.

—Bradley Preber, CEO, Grant Thornton LLP

Introduction

I had a great childhood growing up in Mumbai, India. I moved to Lynchburg, Virginia—an absolutely beautiful town near the Blue Ridge Mountains—to attend college in 1990.

I grew up in a hustling and bustling metropolis with roughly twelve million souls (twenty million now) and then moved to a city of roughly 65,000 (85,000 now) in the American South. I came to the States as an international student, then found employment before getting my green card—I didn't know I was an alien until I came to the States—and eventually became a citizen. I have thoroughly enjoyed my experience and life here in the land of the free. I went to college; earned my MBA; found a career I enjoyed in consulting, knowledge management, and technology; got married and had kids; moved to various cities for different jobs (Cleveland and Boston); and finally settled in Northern Virginia, outside Washington, DC, a city where I felt at home with my wife, Monica, and two sons, Jai and Arjun. I was not a work-aholic, but I was a diligent, efficient corporate guy, a good planner, a fiercely independent and very practical person who wanted to provide enough for my family. Many told me how being practical was my biggest strength. I also loved sports, music, and films (both Bollywood and Hollywood). As a sportsman in my younger days in India, I played competitive badminton and cricket. I loved to run and play racquetball and tennis, and did so whenever I could. I picked up my love of baseball while in Cleveland, and of American football in DC.

When it comes to baseball, I am a Cleveland Indians fan and, recently, a fan of the World Series champions Washington Nationals. As for American football, like many in this region, I remain a huge and optimistic fan of the Washington Redskins (temporary new name: Washington Football Team; soon to have a permanent one)—even if their record for the last twenty years has been dismal.

"Hail to the Redskins" (HTTR)—the fight song of the team I totally believe in!

Why I Wrote This Book

Prior to my stroke, my life was normal and predictable. But on that notable day in January, I suffered a rare, catastrophic hemorrhagic stroke in my cerebellum. On that one fine day, my previous life ended forever, and a new normal set in and has been changing ever since.

"One fine day" means life can and will change for good or bad—whether that change is physical or emotional, big or small, personal or professional, planned or sudden, for anyone rich or poor, Black or white, old or young. The change could be any adversity, such as physical illness, lay-off, divorce, loss of a loved one, the coronavirus pandemic. Good life changes might be marriage, the birth of a child, promotion, or retirement. All these changes alter our life's trajectory and require successful adaptation.

One Fine Day is the story of my recovery, one that took me around the world many times and that encompassed not only the best of Western medicine, technology, and care, but also the best of Eastern holistic healing practices and care. By supplementing cutting-edge Western medical technology with alternate medicines and care practices, we can achieve greater results that contribute to healing the whole person. But I want to stress that you need both. *One Fine Day* presents the way I have used both in my ongoing recovery to have the best chance to heal my mind and body.

My mission is to share how to prepare for your one fine day, embracing whatever tomorrow may hold and living life to the fullest while building it with purpose, meaning, and value. Everything in life is impermanent, and our lives can and will change at any moment, with or without warning. Will you be ready? Will you accept? Will you rejoice?

As hard as it is to embrace a new normal, it is the only choice we have, and acceptance is the key. Self-pity and complaining are not options. It took major tragedies for me to fully realize the one-fine-day message. I don't want anyone else to wait for a tragedy to happen to realize the message fully. I sincerely hope my message in *One Fine Day* serves as a wake-up call that we are all one fine day away from a new normal, however big or small. It reminds you to be grateful and thankful for each day you are here and to not get too carried away or plan too far ahead. I certainly don't want to scare anyone, but to only raise awareness of this and help others to better prepare, physically and emotionally. I certainly wasn't prepared, so I want to share the many experiences and lessons learned from my journey that are helping me heal my mind and body. Life is too short. We all have to tell those we care for that we love them. We need not carry any burdens or grudges, as life can change in an instant. We all should enjoy each and every moment.

So how was I supposed to write a memoir under my condition? I couldn't type with two hands or focus on a computer for an extended time due to my health. Additionally, I was not a writer. But I was determined and motivated to get my message across somehow, as I want my memoir to serve a greater purpose. The benefits far outweigh the pains and challenges of undertaking this project. I found a way to do it by outsourcing the writing part to a professional ghostwriter in the US. I was also not sure if I could revisit the events of the last three and a half years, but in fact found writing about it to be cathartic, which helps my own healing and may well help others. I can honestly say it made me anxious, as I was documenting very openly many personal things in my life.

One Fine Day is an honest memoir written from my

heart. Besides trying both Western and Eastern medicine, I have also made some life changes to assist my healing. As a positive and a fiercely independent person, I want to share as much as I can with others who may also be going through any life changes. It's what we call in business the art of the possible. It provides readers with new ideas, tips, concepts, suggestions, and approaches for what is possible when embracing your new normal, and which worked for me. These decisions should always be made in consultation with professionals. I had no idea what some of my choices were to help me heal. Although my memoir is not a total prescriptive book (i.e. a list of top things to do to face your life changes), it is my sincere hope that the account of my experiences will provide some comfort, information, and inspiration to people facing any life changes—good or bad—and a new normal. If I can touch one other person and shed a little light, it will all be worth it. I am still fighting hard to recover and accept my new normal, and some days are better than others, but my story is a life-saving demonstration of the power of a positive attitude, the power of gratitude, and the strength of diversity and humanity.

My goal is not to preach any particular view, practice, or belief. It is to relate my experiences about the things I have done in my journey. I am very lucky to have survived and grateful for it. Of course you need luck, but a lot of hard work and grit are needed to heal.

My acceptance has increased over time, although I must be honest and say I have not fully accepted everything— I don't think one ever can. As Elizabeth Smart, who was abducted when she was fourteen for nine months from her home in Utah, says, "Ultimately, it's our choices that make us who we are."

One Fine Day is also a letter of gratitude to the hundreds of compassionate caregivers, friends, family, colleagues, and supporters in both my adopted country and my country of birth. From diverse backgrounds—whether they are white, Black, Brown, or any other skin color, local or immigrant, legal or undocumented, rich or poor, educated or uneducated, of different religions, ethnicities, or castes—they aided my recovery and literally saved my life. There is still good in this world no matter what color or nationality you are, what your residence status is, or what economic stratum you come from. I want to highlight the generosity and kindness of these extraordinary people, some of whom were total strangers.

There are bad apples no matter where you are. As is said, "Haters will hate." It is best to ignore them and not let them affect you. In an age where stories of extreme nationalism, polarization, and borders grab many of the headlines, my story is a reminder of our shared humanity and connectivity that goes well beyond politics, nations, and ethnicities. No matter what anyone may say, the real strength of both the United States and India—the world's oldest democracy and the world's largest democracy respectively—lies in their peoples' diversity.

As I walk the reader through my recovery, I will pay homage to all those who have helped me along the way. My life has changed dramatically over the last couple of years. Even though it was life-altering and sudden, I feel lucky—lucky that the paramedics came to me within thirty minutes, lucky I was home and not in a hotel, as I used to travel a lot (I had been in Dallas just the previous week), lucky that I was so close to a hospital, lucky to have had an expert surgeon just starting his ER shift and who specializes in this type of stroke, lucky that the stroke didn't affect the dominant side of my body. I'm lucky all these things lined up, and now I'm lucky to be able to tell my story about my one fine day and help guide the reader a little through their own one fine day, whatever it might be for them and its resulting new normal.

The United States has been good to me and has taught me many things in life, which are helping me in these difficult times. In spite of the various socioeconomic and political challenges the nation faces (What country doesn't?), it is still a beacon of hope for the world. I read somewhere that "equivocation and self-doubt is not the American spirit." How true! *One Fine Day* is written with that philosophy in mind. I am also lucky to have a mother who instilled in me similar values and philosophy.

Chapter Overview

Chapter 1 recounts the events of that one fine day—the day my life changed dramatically—and the following month. Chapter 2 describes the second month after my one fine day and includes my attempt to understand why I was in the hospital and what had happened. Chapter 3 returns me home, where my extensive rehab continues. Chapter 4 describes my first trip to Nimba Nature Cure in India, where I continued my rehab while supplementing it with a number of naturopathic and Eastern holistic healing practices. Chapter 5 takes me back to the States for continuing outpatient rehab with my family, and in chapter 6, I return to India for further rehab. Chapter 7 deals with how my personal and family life changed in ways I never would have expected. Chapters 8 and 9 outline my triumphs, challenges, and adjustments to my new normal, and in chapter 10, I continue to face my ever-changing new normal. Chapter 11 brings my story into the present, reflecting on the journey I've been on and the future I will face.

Each chapter contains inspirational quotes, provides health recovery levels the way I saw them, starting with 0 percent right after my surgery, and ends with lessons I have learned from my journey—I call them Sameerisms.

My Views

Remembering What I Can

I may have missed events, the sequence of events, or names. I have written from what I remember about my experiences, not what I heard from family, friends, doctors, or others. I use third-party accounts sparingly, and only when needed, especially about the time I was in a coma. It's possible I may have missed things. This being said, overall I think I haven't done bad for a guy who lost many brain cells due to a hemorrhage. I wish I could say I remember all this just from memory, but the reality is, a lot is from the daily journal I have kept since Nimba (a habit instilled in me there), emails, text messages, and the like.

Use of Real Names

I debated very much whether to use real or fictitious names for family, friends, and the various health care providers and caretakers in India and the US. I decided to use real names for two main reasons:

1. It just did not feel right using fictitious names. I wanted to thank the many people from diverse backgrounds who aided in my recovery and saved my life.
2. There are too many people in my journey for me to change their names. Having said this, I want to ensure privacy for myself, my family, and friends, and want to avoid sharing anything overly personal. I have no desire whatsoever to air my or anyone's dirty laundry. I want this memoir to be relevant and, hopefully, inspirational to people going through any life changes and the resultant new normal. I use first or last names only, although, in some cases, full name are used when required.

Royalties

A certain portion of whatever royalties I earn from this book will be donated to Inova Health Foundation, a non-profit organization to which I owe my life, and to United Way Worldwide's COVID-19 Community Response and Recovery Fund.

One
Fine
Day

CHAPTER 1

One Fine Day

"No one is so brave that he is not disturbed by something unexpected."

JULIUS CAESAR

Prior to January 31, 2017, my life was chugging along just fine. I had transitioned nicely to my life in the States, had a great job and family, and was well settled. Moving to the States had been a huge cultural shock. I had always wanted to come to the US for higher studies (okay, to be honest, what attracted me more was that I thought life in the States would be like what I saw on TV series like *Miami Vice*, *Dynasty*, and *Dallas*). I was stunned by the Southern hospitality I experienced in Lynchburg, Virginia, my college town. People were just so friendly, polite, and kind in contrast to Mumbai, where they are always on the go, like in New York. Initially, I was skeptical; I thought they wanted something from me. It took me a few days to realize that their hospitality was genuine. I just could not believe it when strangers in an elevator would say, "How are you doing?" or someone on the street would say "Hi" in passing. This concept was foreign to me as an Indian and as a guy from a megalopolis where people generally don't have time to exchange pleasantries with strangers. I thought to myself, "This is the real America." It certainly was not what I had seen on *Miami Vice*, *Dynasty*, *Dallas*, or in Hollywood movies.

The morning of January 31, 2017, began like any normal workday for me. My job at Grant Thornton LLP, a professional services firm, could be done remotely, so my routine had me up early, checking emails on my laptop in the master bedroom. I still remember some of my last emails before my life changed that one fine day. Among the many work-related emails, I clearly recall the ones to my colleague Doug Kalish and my boss, Dave Boland, asking about strategizing and enhancing the digital workspace vision for Grant Thornton. Both are absolute gentlemen, kind and intelligent. I also fondly remember some personal emails that were important to me. I was planning a family trip to Europe for the fall, before my older son, Jai, went to college, and researching the purchase of a pool table for the basement for our younger son, Arjun. Both the boys are good kids, intelligent, and gentle. Monica, my wife, a talented writer and a good cook, was downstairs, going about her own morning routine.

After using the restroom, I was just starting to make some headway with my inbox when, suddenly, my left sinus, below my left eye, started to hurt. My sinuses had always caused me trouble, but never like this—it was throbbing, and the pain was much worse than I'd ever experienced before.

At that moment, Monica came upstairs, and I told her about the severe, throbbing pain. I became dizzy and found I could not sit up straight on the bed. So I just lay down, like a typical man or a typical Indian or both—we generally have a tendency to discount health issues. I figured I would take two Advil and sleep it off. But then I started to sweat. Something was definitely wrong. I knew it and told Monica. There was a history of heart problems in my family, and I figured I was having a heart attack.

Obviously very worried, Monica called 9-1-1 and my doctor, at the time Dr. Pappas, to see what he thought we should do. The paramedics arrived very quickly. God bless Monica for calling them, and the paramedics for coming immediately. That might have saved my life because when it comes to strokes, time is critical. When they arrived upstairs, they checked my vitals and symptoms. My blood pressure and my electrocardiogram were normal, but the throbbing pain, dizziness, and sweating continued at full strength. Since my vitals were normal, the paramedics could not figure out what was wrong. They thought I might have a severe migraine headache, so they decided—lucky for me—to take me to the hospital. I, however, was convinced that I was having a coronary and insisted that they check my heart as they were taking me downstairs. (This, by the way, is also a very Indian thing to do: give directions!) I remember the paramedic saying, "Sir, your heart is fine."

They took me downstairs and loaded me into the ambulance, where it was nice and warm, a feeling always welcome during a DC winter, especially to a man from India. I remember Monica's and Jai's worried faces. (We had not awakened Arjun, who was quite young, as we did not want him to see his dad this way.) Then I remember Jai saying, "Dad, whatever it is, we will face it," or something to that effect. The ambulance doors closed, and soon after that, I passed out.

The Missing Month

The next thirty days or so went by without my consciousness or awareness, as I was in a medically induced coma in the ICU. Only later would I begin to piece together the story, based on Monica's and Jai's accounts. I found out many of my close friends had come to the ICU to provide us help and support.

Fortunately, Inova Fairfax Hospital was only two or three miles from our home. I arrived and was admitted to the emergency room. They could not make sense of my symptoms. The doctor assigned to me asked me if there was anything else happening to me. I don't remember this, but I apparently said that it felt like my left hand was floating in the air.

As soon as they heard that, they immediately took me for an MRI or CAT scan (I'm not sure which). The tests revealed that a blood vessel had burst in my cerebellum, and I'd suffered a hemorrhagic stroke. With blood collecting in my brain, I was rushed to the operating room for emergency surgery. It was my good luck that a neurosurgeon who specializes in back-of-the-brain bleeds, Dr. Nilesh Vyas, was just then coming on shift. Within an hour or so, I was on the operating table and undergoing a left sub-occipital craniectomy and hematoma evacuation for a ruptured cerebral cavernous malformation (abnormality), which was the cause of my massive stroke and hemorrhage.

I awoke, barely, in the ICU. I was not sure when I'd gotten there or how much time had elapsed. I regained some consciousness for the first time since I'd passed out in the ambulance, but for some reason, I thought I was in Baltimore. I was in the midst of an evaluation with a physical therapist, a fellow Indian, who was assessing my musculature and strength. I asked him his name.

"I am Gopal," he said in a soft voice.

"Where in India are you from?" I asked.

"Mumbai," he said.

I knew Mumbai quite well. "Which part of Mumbai are you from?" I asked.

"Govandi," he said.

Mumbai is huge, but I knew exactly where the suburb of Govandi was, and I told him so. I think he was genuinely surprised to hear that. I didn't know it at the time, but this was to be the first heartfelt connection I would experience with one of my caregivers. These interactions with warm people would span the coming years and stretch across two continents. Gopal finished his evaluation, gave me a friendly good-bye, and went about his rounds. I remember him being soft-spoken, intelligent, and an absolute gentleman. That experience was to be the only true memory I'd retain of the "real" world for the duration of the month I spent in the coma while my brain repaired itself.

My only other memory from that time is a long series of bizarre and vivid hallucinations. In one, I was flying to India with President Trump and Vice President Pence to broker a meeting with Mr. Balasaheb Thackeray, a leader of a right-leaning political party in my home state of Maharashtra. (Mr. Thackeray, incidentally, had died years earlier.) In the hallucination, I was flying on a Trump Shuttle with the president and his wife, his son Barron, and the boy's babysitter. The shuttle landed at Mr. Thackeray's beachside bungalow in Mumbai, and then we all went to a dinner party. Mrs. Pence had brought a dog along. I asked someone, "Is this Debbie's dog?" (Although I had no idea if her name was Debbie or if she even had a dog! In my hallucination, Debbie was her name. Her name is Karen, I've since discovered, but the Pences would indeed get a dog—but not until later that year.)

In yet another hallucination, my damaged brain tossed together a whole pile of random elements. I was in an ambulance and, for some reason, traveling through Philadelphia, a city I'd visited a few times in the past few years for work but had no real connection with. On the ambulance ride, I was accompanied by my brother-in-law, Sumir, my sister-in-law, Arti, and their daughter, Shivani, who live in Arizona. I was scolding Shivani for something, which is completely uncharacteristic of me—but there it was, one of my few "memories" of that February. There were many other details in the hallucinations of my trips that have become fuzzy, but these two are firmly entrenched in my mind, as if they had been real.

Later, I asked Dr. Vyas why I so vividly remember these hallucinations, and he said it was because of the strong medications I'd been given during the surgery. I probably had seen the therapy dogs that had come to the ICU, so maybe one of them made it into my hallucination as Debbie's. And Arti had come to visit me in the hospital, so perhaps some part of my brain noticed she was there and folded Sumir and Shivani in as well.

Beyond those hallucinations, the next thing I was aware of was lying in an ambulance. I remember a cold breeze passing through the cabin—anyone who has visited the nation's capital in winter can attest to such frigid temperatures. I couldn't speak or move—and it would be some time before I could—but I eventually came to learn that I was on the Capital Beltway, on my way from Inova Fairfax Hospital, where I'd spent nearly the entire month in a coma, to Inova Mount Vernon Hospital. This was where I'd undergo postoperative care and begin a rehabilitation process that would prove to be one of the most difficult yet uplifting and transformative processes I'd ever experienced.

The following chapters describe that process—still ongoing—which took me around the world multiple times and continues to bring me into contact with caregivers and supporters who have confirmed my belief in a goodness in humanity that transcends race, socioeconomics, and national borders. By looking beyond these surface differences, I've learned that amazing things are possible. I'm a living testament to this. Before I could gain that perspective, though, I had to begin with the task of figuring out what had happened to me—no easy task, considering my complete helplessness upon emerging from my coma.

• • •

"Anything can happen. Anything happens all the time."

—ROSE BYRNE

Health Recovery Level

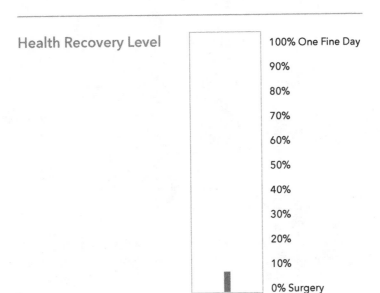

	100% One Fine Day
	90%
	80%
	70%
	60%
	50%
	40%
	30%
	20%
	10%
	0% Surgery

SAMEERISM • Count your blessings—each and every day—and constantly remind yourself of this.

CHAPTER 2

Why Me?

"I never question God. Sometimes I say, 'Why me?
Why do I have such a hard life? Why do I have this
disease? Why do I have siblings who died?' But then
I think and say, 'Why not me?'"

MATTIE STEPANEK

"What the hell happened?"

That was the question that began to form in my mind after I emerged from my coma. I felt like a rug had been pulled out from under me. I came to in an ambulance that was taking me on a forty-minute ride to the rehabilitation unit at Inova Mount Vernon Hospital in Alexandria, Virginia. You can imagine how frightening it must have been to wake up on a stretcher and have no idea how you got there or where you were going. I was scared, yes, but more than anything, I was confused. Sorting out what had happened to me would take some time. Accepting it would take even longer.

My memories of arriving and getting situated at Inova Mount Vernon are sporadic. And my memories of my thirty days in the ICU at Inova Fairfax Hospital were almost non-existent. Besides my interaction with Gopal, I vaguely recall three other things: my favorite music being played in the ICU (Lord Ganesh prayers—*aarti*—by Amitabh Bachchan, my favorite Bollywood superstar); Dr. Djurkovic, the ICU doctor (like many others, we referred to him as Dr. D.), and Boo-Boo the ICU attendant.

Slowly, my awareness of the world began to fall back into place, thanks to the super care of the hospital staff and the loving attention of my family and friends. We were truly blessed to be surrounded by friends from diverse backgrounds who helped us tremendously. Obviously, it was great to see Monica next to me, but I also loved seeing my childhood friend Anil, who lives in Boston and is a good-looking and extremely fit guy. Anil was my state-level badminton doubles partner in Mumbai and has been a close friend ever since. Anil was visiting Mumbai when I had the stroke. As Monica knew Anil and I were close, and she and the boys were also fond of him, she called him to come to Virginia to help us. He dropped everything and came to help us and stayed at our home until early May. God bless him for being there for us. That is indeed a true friend.

The borderline between waking and dreaming was hazy. My strange and vivid hallucinations continued, especially reoccurring ones of President Trump. In one, I continued to think I was in India with him, even as Monica told me that my mother and sister were flying in from India for a visit. I was perplexed and asked her, "Why are they flying to Mumbai? They live here." Monica responded that I was in Virginia all this time, not in India, and that my mom and sister were coming to see me. Very strange, I thought— probably the result of too much cable news over the years before the stroke, especially during the 2016 elections!

Monica was the first person who tried to explain what had happened to me. On one hand, she wanted to tell me all she knew about my stroke and my month in the ICU. On the other hand, she was trying to be careful not to make things worse by upsetting me. I could see the concern on her face and hear the hesitation in her voice. She gave me some information, but I'm not sure it really sank in. One of the biggest mysteries to me was how the heck I had a stroke without any warning or symptoms, and after having had a complete physical just a few days before. We got answers from Dr. Vyas. Apparently, there are two types of strokes. The most common is a lifestyle stroke (related to weight, smoking, diet, and the like), and the other is genetic. I had this genetic cerebral vascular abnormality from birth. This condition, which is rare, affects a very small population in the US. According to the *Handbook of Neurosurgery* by Dr. Mark S. Greenberg, this abnormality develops in about 3,300 to 58,800 people in the United States. But when it results in a hemorrhage, as in my case, it is even rarer—it only happens to 86 to 1,730 people per year in the US. Many of those people die. I am extremely lucky and thankful to have survived. Not all cavernous abnormalities result in a hemorrhage. Many people have this abnormality, but not everyone experiences a rupture as I did. From what I understood, I was born with this vascular abnormality and suffered a devastating hemorrhagic stroke. It could have happened anytime when I was a child, teen, young adult, or later. It affected my hand and leg on the left side. If it had been right sub-occipital, then it would have affected my right side, which would have been more disastrous, as I am right-handed. My doctors also said that had the vascular abnormality been a millimeter to the right, I would have been paralyzed for life.

At this point, I was still probably two or three weeks away from being able to speak easily, so I couldn't ask all the questions I wanted to. I found out from Monica that I had had not one, but two brain surgeries, the second six days after the first one. On February 5, Monica saw that my face was pale and told the ICU doctors. My vitals were normal, so the doctors did not seem alarmed. But Monica knew something was wrong, so she again expressed her concern, and this time the doctors listened to her instincts. They checked me out further and realized that I needed another surgery. (Sometimes your instincts are better than science.)

Monica also told me how the good folks from Grant Thornton delivered food to the ICU and our home, and that our kind neighbors, family, and friends had helped to start a food chain for us. Maria Izurieta, the ex CFO of my previous company, 3Pillar Global, happened to be in the ICU during the same time visiting her mom, and saw Monica freezing in the ICU and got her a blanket. My aunt Dr. Smita, who lives in Maryland, talked to me in Marathi, my mother tongue, as doctors wanted someone to speak to me in the language I spoke while growing up. I found out from Jai about Tom Brady's (the elite quarterback for the New England Patriots football team) historic twenty-five-point comeback in the Super Bowl. I was undergoing my second brain surgery that day, so I have absolutely no recollection whatsoever for a long time after. If someone had told me that the New England Patriots won the Super Bowl, I would have said, "Big deal." But they were down twenty-five points in the fourth quarter of the game and won in overtime—totally unreal. Folks who follow American football know exactly what I am talking about. I can go on and on regarding this for two pages or more, but I won't to keep sanity for others. Those who know us, know that Jai and I are close and talk about a lot of things, especially sports, and they were not surprised about this conversation between us.

Obviously, I knew there was something wrong with me. Even with the aid of a walker, I couldn't get out of bed during my first few days at Inova Mount Vernon. I felt very weak. My left side was almost paralyzed—I could barely move my left hand and leg. Yet the little bit of motion I was capable of was important. Monica told me that Gopal had tried hard and hoped that I would respond to his commands in the ICU by showing some movement in my left hand. If I did, he could recommend me to Dr. Vyas for local inpatient rehab. They had been prepared to send me to a nursing home in Atlanta if I couldn't show any movement.

In the end, I somehow was able to give a thumbs-up sign with my left hand, and it was enough for them to send me to Inova Mount Vernon. That small triumph was a big first step in my recovery journey.

My month-long stay at Inova Mount Vernon would result in a series of little victories in an ongoing battle that continues even as I write this. Beyond the struggle to overcome what the massive stroke had done to my body was the need to repair my spirit. Understanding what had happened was hard enough, but there were also the visible signs and marks of surgeries on my body: a big incision made at the back of my head for the craniectomy, a big mark on my throat due to a tracheostomy, a feeding tube in my belly, and injection and IV marks on my hand.

On top of that, I was fighting anger and depression. As I grew more aware of what I had been through and what was ahead, I kept asking myself, "Why me? Why am I suffering?" and "Why does my family have to suffer?"

The center of my world during that month was my hospital room. It was located on an upper floor, facing an open area. The view was fantastic, perfect for recovery, but it was so bright that the light kept giving me headaches. The important thing, though, was that I was rarely, if ever, alone. I would wake up to find someone sitting in the chair next to my bed: a doctor, a nurse, Monica, a family member, a friend. I remember their constant presence and conversations with me. They gave me the strength to heal.

A steady stream of friends kept arriving to help us, which was huge for Monica and me. It was heartwarming to see them all, especially my close friend since fourth grade Kedar, and his wife, Vrinda, from New Jersey; my college friend Mak and his wife, Meghana, (also from New Jersey); Lydia and Chandu, good friends who we knew for a while, and Brian and Valerie, good friends whose son, Sam, was Jai's childhood friend.

One night it was also wonderful to see my buddies Ron, Sal, and Luis. We called ourselves Los Cuotes, "the buddies." We had all gone to Spain together in 2016 for one of my most memorable trips. I call them my brothers from another mother. We are truly blessed to be good friends: two Latinos, an Indian, and a white guy. I can't thank all of them enough for their kindness and friendship.

I found out from Kedar that my situation had been so dire in the ICU that even Vrinda, not religious like me, resorted to reading the *pothi*, a Hindu religious text, which means "a book or manuscript." It was a caring thing for her to do. Many religious people, including Kedar, read the *pothi* daily. Over the years, many Indians have assumed I am a religious person since my last name traditionally indicates a person from a hardcore Hindu Brahmin family. But in fact I don't believe much in any organized religion, nor did my father or his mother.

The Inova Mount Vernon Hospital's medical staff didn't hold back in explaining what was ahead, which, as a practical person, I truly appreciated. They told me that, while rehab typically gets patients back on track over time, nobody could say whether I would be able to walk or function normally again, and if so, when and how much. They didn't know how my recovery would go. All they could say was that it would be a long journey. Fortunately, I didn't have to travel it alone.

My mom and my sister, Sunita, flew in from India for a weeklong visit. Like Monica, they seemed to be in a state of shock but tried to stay composed. My mother, a strong person, had raised me to face difficult situations with a positive attitude. Even so, seeing her son in a hospital bed without any real idea if he'd ever be well again must've been extremely hard on her. It was equally shocking for Sunita—she, being an extremely gentle person, must have found it hard.

Of course, Jai and Arjun came to see me. They tried to be strong, but I could see the fear in their faces. I can only imagine what went through their minds when they saw their dad lying flat on his back in a hospital bed, unable to get up. Although it was nice to see my boys, the question of why we all had to suffer kept coming to me, and I felt terribly sorry for them.

It was Kedar who got me to accept the truth about my situation. We had been close ever since growing up in Mumbai. I told him in plain terms that I was finding it hard to accept what had happened to me. He said, "You want proof?"

"Absolutely," I said.

At that point, he hesitatingly took out a photograph he'd taken of me in the ICU in Fairfax. There I was, stretched out with all kinds of tubes and wires connected to me. Once I saw that, I fully believed and realized what the doctors and Monica had already told me. Because I had no memory of what had happened, it just didn't seem real until I saw that

photo. Now I believed it. As they say, "Seeing is believing."
It was a breakthrough for me.

I had grown a long, thick beard during my stay at the
ICU, as obviously I was not able to shave. I think it was
shocking for Monica and my boys, especially, to see me this
way, so I was grateful when Anil and my brother-in-law
Sumir (who had flown in from Arizona) brought an electric razor and shaved me. They had to struggle a bit to get
the job done. I don't think they had ever shaved someone's
beard before. I was grateful, and it helped me look and feel
a little more like my old self.

The Inova Mount Vernon medical staff was truly ex-
ceptional. The main physician, Dr. Gisolfi, oversaw my care
and rehab. He was intelligent, competent, and reassuring.
He had more than fifty years of experience in that center.
My therapists, Ashley, Sam, Heather, and Lori, as well as an
intern from Manassas, were there to keep my recovery on
track. I always felt in good hands. All the nurses were kind
and awesome, from the locals, Carla and Claire, to many
others who were from the African continent. There were
just too many to remember their names. (Another Indian
thing—typically, we tend not to offer a compliment quickly,
unless you are the boss, in which case the compliment is
usually not genuine.) I especially connected with Dan, one
of the night nurses, a positive and jovial person. We were
both fans of the Washington Redskins, the National Football
League (NFL), and sports in general, so that gave us plenty
to talk about.

The rehab process was not easy. Starting the various

therapies proved challenging and often frustrating. I learned there were different types of therapies: physical, focused on developing my strength and stamina; occupational, focused on improving my ability to do day-to-day activities, such as walking and standing; speech, focused on my ability to talk and swallow, as well as my memory and cognitive skills. I had always been a sportsman. I used to train hard and could run for an hour, but now my left leg was so weak that I couldn't walk five steps by myself. My left arm and hand were just as impaired. At the time, I didn't see how lucky I was that it was my left side that was affected. I was angry at the injustice of what I was going through. The question still haunted my mind: "Why me?"

Every morning, I was fearful of not passing urine, since the nurses would have no choice but to use the catheter, which was extremely painful. I called it the required evil. I started getting used to adult diapers, though.

Fully regaining my ability to speak was a long process as well. The doctors had told me that following a stroke of this magnitude in the cerebellum, my main issue would be balance and motor control. They also said that the muscles in my jaw and throat had been affected, which in turn would influence some of my ability to talk or swallow. My cognitive ability or memory, however, were not affected. A speech therapist started giving me exercises, and I slowly made progress. The same was true with swallowing. Initially, I couldn't handle anything firmer than mashed potatoes. Gradually, I moved up to semi-soft foods like macaroni and cheese. I also fondly remember eating *sheera*, a traditional delicacy from my part of the world sent by Chandu's mom. It is soft, so I could eat it. The pace of improvement was reasonably steady, but the doctors had no idea whether I'd be in the hospital for one month or two. Every day was a rehab day, and I had to keep moving forward.

With physical therapy and occupational therapy, my body strength increased gradually. I am not sure when it was, but I took some steps with a walker, then started using it regularly, which felt great after thirty days in bed. It also felt awesome to take a bath for the first time with the help and under the watchful eyes of the therapist. Then I started taking regular baths, although sitting on a stool and under supervision of the therapist.

By the end of the month, I was able to stay on my feet with the aid of a walker. The doctors felt I was ready to go home. They removed the feeding tube from my stomach. It was extremely painful to take it out, but they had no other way to do it. There was no big send-off, but many people on the staff did stop by to say good-bye. Monica and Anil came to get me, and the nurse Carla helped me into the car. I was finally heading home after sixty days in the hospital. I was grateful to have survived and just be alive, but so ready to go home. My journey back to health was just beginning, of course. I left Inova Mount Vernon thankful for the excellent care I'd received, but I was still pissed. "Why me?" and "Why us?" continued to hound me. I had come to understand what had happened to me. But there were many more questions I would need to answer.

The quest to learn and heal would take me around

the world and deep inside myself. When I arrived home, I carried with me a full realization of what I'd been through and how far I still had to go.

• • •

"Don't think about tomorrow, day after that, day after that. Think about today. Win today. Let's go 1-0, and if we can do that, we will go 1-0 tomorrow, and then 1-0 next day, next day, and next day. And if we have enough of those, we will get to where we want."

—DAVEY MARTINEZ, Manager of the 2019 World Series champions Washington Nationals

Health Recovery Level

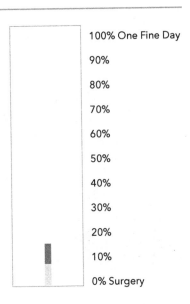

100% One Fine Day

90%

80%

70%

60%

50%

40%

30%

20%

10%

0% Surgery

SAMEERISM • Don't be tempted to compare your recovery with that of others. Keep in mind that every situation and adversity is different. Learn to accept that you will heal at your own pace, and that is perfectly okay.

CHAPTER 3

My New Reality

*"Every day is a gift, which is why
they call it the present."*

ALFRED HITCHCOCK

Home at last! After two months in the hospital, I returned
to our townhouse in Dunn Loring, Virginia, ready to enter
the next phase of my healing. I thought to myself, "It's a
miracle that I am still alive and have returned home." I felt
excited and overwhelmed about being home. I'd missed out
on two months of time with my wife and children, and there
was much to catch up on. It was a happy day.

Monica helped me from the car into a wheelchair she
had bought and took me into the house through the garage
entrance. She'd created a living space for me with a new bed
in our finished basement, which functioned as our home's
first floor, making my transition back home as comfortable

as possible. We'd been using part of the basement as an office and a play area for the kids; it had a half-bath, and because it was a walkout basement, there was plenty of natural light. If I needed anything, I could call upstairs to Monica.

My new reality had begun, but facing it was not easy. I kept asking myself why a young man of forty-seven years found himself sleeping in a basement like someone's elderly relative. Yes, I was back home and with my family and was very grateful, but things obviously weren't the same as when I'd left. I kept thinking of metrics to measure how I used to be and how I was now. I had been going 100 miles an hour before the stroke. Now I was reduced to twenty miles an hour at best.

I waffled between thinking I would go back to my old normal soon and wondering if I could ever be the same again. I could only think in extremes. Mostly, I was just pissed off.

With these thoughts raging in my head, I settled into a daily routine. For diversion, I listened to a lot of music; it made me feel good. I also started to listen to some spiritual recordings. I would tune out the religious pieces if there were any, but I appreciated the spiritual messages. As I listened to them, the key was to keep an open mind. It's astonishing how spiritual they were when I took out the religious connotations. Two of my favorites were Joel Olsteen and Sadhguru. Many people find these two figures controversial, but I really like their spiritual messages. I also tried to sleep as much as I could, but my crazy hallucinations continued, and the border between waking and dreaming continued to be hazy. I don't remember them as vividly as I do the ones with President Trump in them. Being a hopeless news junkie, I continued to watch news on TV.

I ate twice a day. Monica cooked my meals and brought them downstairs to me. I ate a lot of soups, salads, and vegetables prepared mostly Indian-style. We also ordered some carryout. I was grateful for Monica's care, and overall, I think I was a good patient. But I felt badly that I had to be so dependent upon my wife. I had always been an independent person, a trait I get from my mother and grandmother, and being in the United States had taught me how to be fiercely autonomous. Now I had to rely completely on my wife. I knew Monica was trying to be as strong as possible, but I noticed the strain on her face. I couldn't make her responsibilities easier, which only contributed to my frustration.

Fortunately, she had help from Anil, who stayed with us for two months. At the time, he was between jobs in Boston, so he moved into Jai's bedroom and became a member of our family. Anil helped Monica with grocery shopping and other errands, including driving around. A fitness fanatic, Anil also helped me with exercises as I slowly regained strength. I could see on his face that he was heartbroken over what had happened to me. Over time, I started to talk to him about what I was going through mentally, but we had been so close for so long that I didn't have to say much for him to understand. Anil's presence was huge for us. I am grateful and thankful for all his help.

I wanted to take an active part in my sons' lives again.

Jai was in the middle of deciding where to attend college when I came home from the hospital. I was glad that we had gone through all the college possibilities before my stroke. Now he had narrowed his choice down to two universities. It was frustrating that I couldn't help him with the final applications. We did talk about what university was right for him. I explained to Jai that while both were good universities, one of them was definitely cheaper as it was in-state.

Anil took Jai on visits to both campuses. He said to me, "Let Jai decide which one he likes the best." I agreed with him, but being pragmatic, I thought that if everything was equal, an in-state school was the right choice. In the end, Jai did choose the in-state school on his own. He drove the entire process, making me feel very proud.

Although Jai and I would talk a little about the challenges I faced, it was different with my younger son, Arjun. I tried to be as normal as possible in front of him, which was difficult. I would be lying in bed in the basement when he came home from school, and it made me feel bad. In general, he and I didn't talk that much about my health situation. I didn't want him to feel his life had to change because of what had happened to me.

I was so glad when our friend Shirley volunteered to organize a Harry Potter–themed party for Arjun's birthday. He loves Harry Potter, and we knew it would mean a lot to him. Monica and I stayed in the basement and gave Arjun the space to have a great time with his friends. Shirley really outdid herself. I could see how happy Arjun was, and for this, I will be ever grateful to her. Also, I will be ever grateful to my cousins Neal and Priya, who one evening took the boys for their favorite activity: the Escape Room.

My rehab program continued with home therapy. My physical therapist, Patty, came to see me once or twice a week. She had a bubbly personality, and I felt good just talking to her. She also talked with Monica and made her feel better too. We gradually increased the use of weights for my hands and legs. I still do these exercises today.

Larry was my occupational therapist and would also come once or twice a week. He was a big guy, strong, jovial, and patient, and I enjoyed talking with him about events in the news or whatever came to mind. His family had gone through the tragic loss of a loved one, but he was positive and inspirational. We laughed a lot and that helped make the exercises go more smoothly. As a therapist, Larry concentrated on helping me walk with the use of a walker before he helped me take my first steps using a cane. I knew I could lean on the big guy if I stumbled along the way.

If Larry was outgoing, Erin, the speech therapist, was the quiet one. I was able to speak by this time, though I often talked in a sort of mumbo-jumbo with words missing from my sentences. Erin focused on improving my speech and my ability to swallow. She also gave me puzzles to do to improve my cognitive skills. Although this therapy was less intensive than the other physical exercises, it was more tiring mentally. I had to stick with it if I was going to improve.

I also had a home aide named Pearl, who helped me bathe and do other things I still couldn't do for myself. Like Patty, Larry, and Erin, she was kind and nurturing, but I found it difficult to have someone outside my family help me with personal functions like bathing. As this wasn't comfortable for me, we stopped using her.

One more person needs to be mentioned here: Sam the barber. I had been getting my hair cut at his shop for about fifteen years prior to my stroke. Sangar (his real name) is from the Kurdish region of northern Iraq and came to the US in 2007. For those who don't know about the Kurds—which I didn't until Sam told me—they are an ethnic people scattered across southeastern Turkey, northwestern Iran, northern Iraq, and northern Syria; many of them dream of founding an independent Kurdistan. The Kurds have their own language and culture. They were in the news in October 2019 when the US began withdrawing its troops from Syria. Sam is about thirty years old, a good-looking guy who is a hard worker and very customer oriented. I teased him a lot because he was still single. I would tell him, "If you go back to Iraq, they will get you married there." Sam's not talkative and speaks in broken English, but we still have great conversations. I'd say we have a real bond.

After I had returned home, Jai contacted Sam and said, "Dad had a stroke and can't come in for haircuts."

Sam told him, "Well, I'll come over there and cut his hair."

Next thing I knew, he came over and gave me a haircut as well as a shave. I wanted to pay him, but he said, "No, no, I won't take any money. When you get better, you can pay me." What a kind gesture on Sam's part.

So many people were there for me in those early months

back home. I stayed in regular touch with my boss, Dave, who kept reassuring me I would get better. I received letters and emails from many people at Grant Thornton to let me know I wasn't forgotten. I was especially touched when I got an email from the then-CEO of Grant Thornton, Mike McGuire. He had found out from Dave about my condition and progress. It was amazing to me that, although Mike and I didn't know each other, he was concerned about me and reached out to offer his sincere best wishes. Here was a CEO of an 8,000-employee company, genuinely concerned for one of his employees. This was not just a nice corporate thing for him to do, and ever since, Mike has sent me numerous messages of encouragement and support. What a leader, what a great human being. In this day and age, his kind of genuine leadership is hard to find. Mike later retired from Grant Thornton, and we still keep in touch.

I was also touched when my colleague Chris Steinhardt, who was suffering from terminal cancer and going through treatments with amazing grace and strength, sent me get-well cards and messages. Chris had been highly instrumental in orienting me to Grant Thornton. Here was a man going through hell himself yet being very nice and supportive to me.

My friend Meghana and my sister-in-law Arti visited from out of town to help Monica and me. They brought us positive energy. Many friends and visitors came over to see how I was doing. There were small but meaningful times to share with them. I hope they all know how much these moments meant to me.

My doctors and therapists had advised that reading books would help heal my brain, so Rahul—a kind and gentle person who had recently married Monica's cousin Shelley—came by to read to me. I was thankful and enjoyed the reading sessions. One of the books he chose from his collection was a lengthy biography of Emperor Shivaji, the seventeenth-century warrior and founder of the Maratha Kingdom, which eventually became the state of Maharashtra, my native state in western India. I vaguely knew his story but few details. Rahul is from the north of India. It made me smile to think that it took a North Indian Punjabi like Rahul to help a Maharashtrian like me learn about the great Shivaji. It's like a French person reading about Viking explorers to a Norwegian. I think we got about halfway through the book. Besides helping me, the important thing was that Rahul and I got to spend some good times together.

I was gaining body strength, could walk using the walker regularly, and could use the toilet on my own, although I continued using adult diapers. Yet I kept asking myself, "Why me?" and "Why does my family have to suffer?" Though denial and depression were constant, for the first time, I started to gradually accept where I was in my recovery. As best as I could tell, I was about 10 percent better than I had been in March in terms of accepting my new reality.

As April turned into May, my private monthly long-term disability (LTD) benefits kicked in. I can't stress enough how important it is to enroll in it. It has kept me afloat. I believe some companies auto-enroll their employees, but in others you have to elect the option as you do with health, dental, and 401(k) benefits. I am lucky I had elected that option during open enrollment and grateful that Grant Thornton had an excellent LTD policy. I actually didn't realize that I had selected it. Thank God I did.

I still thought I would be back at work by July or August. It was hard to let go of the sense that I could make this happen. The bottom line was I could not believe that I was still in this state. I was the kind of person who set goals and met them by a certain date. I could not do that while recovering from this massive stroke. Learning to accept that I had to heal at my own pace wasn't easy.

I took stock of where I was. I don't recall exactly when I moved upstairs to sleep in our master bedroom, but it made me feel like I was getting back to my old normal. I still had my challenges, such as figuring out how to maneuver the wheelchair. I needed Monica's help to dress. I was able to walk up and down the stairs by using the handrail and could take a shower sitting on a stool. My left side remained weak, so I did more tasks with my right hand. This prevented me from doing anything in the kitchen, doing the laundry, or loading the dishwasher, though I could make coffee using Keurig K-Cups. I was able to use my laptop and cellphone a little, which kept me in touch with the outside world.

Overall, I was experiencing the typical effects of a stroke. Fortunately, my cognitive abilities were not impaired. I did suffer from nystagmus, a condition that affects vision, depth perception, and balance. My eyes felt dry. My appetite was good, and I could eat whatever Monica made at home or ordered in. My coffee intake was restricted to two or three cups of decaffeinated a day. Through it all, I somehow kept my sense of humor. I had to.

Monica took me to see Dr. Vyas for a pair of follow-up visits in April and May. After checking to see if there was any new bleeding in my brain, he told me that everything looked good and to keep doing rehab therapy. Dr. Vyas and his assistant, Stacia, left me feeling reassured and hopeful, but they couldn't tell me when I'd fully recover. There was a path for me to follow, but no way to know when my journey to health would be complete. I can't thank them enough for their help.

I noted the milestones I had reached on that path to wellness. Around the end of April, Monica and our friend Lydia—originally from Germany and an extremely kind person—took me on a neighborhood outing in my wheelchair. It was a beautiful spring day in Northern Virginia, and the first time I'd been outside since I'd come home. I wished that day I could have walked on my own power. Still, it felt good to enjoy the sunshine and breathe fresh spring air. Lydia had helped Monica and me a lot after my stroke. She has been there for us from day one. A true friend indeed!

I am not sure exactly when my insane hallucinations stopped, but they did over time as the effects of the drugs started to wear off. I believe by June they had slowly stopped. I had exhausted the home therapy visits covered by my health insurance, so I began a program of outpatient therapy at Inova Fairfax Hospital. Monica took me to around sixty appointments through the end of August, which included continuation of physical, occupational, and speech therapy. I felt bad that Monica had to take me in the wheelchair each time we went for therapy. I wished there were other options I could explore.

I joked with my therapists by asking questions like, "Do you have any magic pill to reduce my dizziness?" One of the things they taught me during therapy was how to load a dishwasher. I didn't think I needed to learn how to because I never thought I would have to do it that much; but later on, this training was extremely helpful. Never say never, I guess. Around this time, I completed speech therapy, a real victory for me.

I also transitioned from Dr. Vyas to Dr. Suneetha Manem, a neurologist. Like Dr. Vyas, she was intelligent and good.

Monica cautiously suggested that I talk to a psychologist to help with my healing. She knew I was not comfortable talking to a third party about what I was going through. Being an analytical and data-driven person, I had never thought that this kind of "touchy-feely" stuff was essential, and I had discounted it. Monica said to try it and only continue it if I felt comfortable. She found a clinical psychologist, Dr. Susan Ammerman, through her network and scheduled an initial evaluation appointment. Over time, I developed trust with Dr. Susan, and she helped my healing. I still see her today.

Whether your ailment is big or small, physical or emotional, personal or professional, I highly recommend talking to a professional psychologist.

In a work environment, the staff of the HR department can serve that purpose, as, generally, they are good at listening to their employees. I had discounted this before my stroke, but I know now how it can be important. This newfound insight of mine was music to some of my dear friends who are HR professionals, as over the years I had kidded with them that this kind of "soft stuff" beyond logic and data was not essential in organizations. Now I knew how valuable this kind of interaction could be.

It was also during this time that Anil's wife, Aparna,

a sweet and bubbly person who I also knew from my bad-minton days, told me about Nimba, a naturopathy center in Gujarat, India. She had gone there for a few days for rejuvenation and had been impressed by what they had to offer. People who went to Nimba ranged from those seeking relaxation to those with health issues. Aparna told me that the facilities were nice and that they offered yoga and energy healing in addition to physical therapy. There was an Ayurvedic doctor on staff. She thought I should check them out.

I considered the idea, but I had my doubts that Nimba could really help me. Monica suggested that I talk to the doctor on staff and go from there. It sounded like a good suggestion, so we arranged a conference call between me, Monica, Aparna, and Dr. Shyamaraj Nidugala, Nimba's chief medical officer. I told Dr. Shyam, as we call him, about my medical condition. I let him know upfront that I didn't wish to come to Nimba and just do yoga and other naturopathy treatments. I wanted to continue doing a full rehab program. He said that Nimba was a holistic facility that offered physical therapy and energy healing along with yoga and massages. Once I heard that, I took the idea of going there more seriously.

Even though I was from India, I had never been that interested in traditional Indian health practices, nor had they been as renowned during my childhood as they are now. I can certainly say yoga is much "cooler" now than it was decades ago, as it is more accepted both in India and the West. I just wouldn't listen back then. Now, I thought it might be time to reconsider and try it in addition to Western medicine.

It still took some convincing for me to go to Nimba. Although it provided holistic treatments, massages, board and lodging, full-time help, and more, and was much more reasonably priced than anything like it in the States, I didn't want to be away from Monica and the boys for an extended period of time. I also felt I would certainly be staying with strangers and embarking on treatments I didn't fully believe in. It was a tough decision, but one I had to make. Finally, two things made me decide to make the trip. The first was I did not want to be more of a burden to Monica. The second was the rising medical costs I faced at home, so it made sense to seek ongoing rehab in India. I did check out a couple of facilities in the States, but they didn't make sense financially. I told Monica that I would give Nimba a try for two or three weeks, and extend my stay longer if it was helping me. Monica wholeheartedly agreed with my decision.

Kedar agreed to escort me all the way to Nimba. I started to call this trip my offshore rehab 1.0. Nimba aided me in my recovery, but it did more than that. What occurred there turned out to be a life-changing experience.

• • •

"We are still masters of our fate. We are still captains of our souls."

—WINSTON CHURCHILL

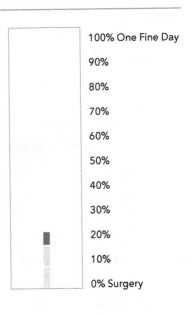

Health Recovery Level

100% One Fine Day

90%

80%

70%

60%

50%

40%

30%

20%

10%

0% Surgery

SAMEERISM

- You have no choice but to play the hand you are dealt. When life hands you lemons, make lemonade, as they say. You cannot "play the victim" beyond a certain time. It's okay to pity yourself initially, but that has to stop quickly so you can slowly begin to accept your new reality and eventually your new normal.

- Take ownership of your decisions. There may be ideas and suggestions from various people who mean well, but at the end of the day, you have to evaluate those and decide what route you want to pursue.

- Use the help of a clinical psychologist to supplement your healing. It helps.

CHAPTER 4

In Search of
a Magic Pill

*"One of the first conditions of happiness is that
the link between Man and Nature shall not be broken."*

LEO TOLSTOY

As we got ready for our trip, Monica helped pack my stuff. This was the first time since I'd moved to the States that I wasn't bringing any goodies back to my friends and family in India. My bags were now filled with "goodies" such as adult diapers, medications, a folding cane, and other items for my medical condition. Monica also wanted to pack a transporter (a light wheelchair) for me to take. I was not keen on the idea, as I thought that Nimba would have wheelchairs. She convinced me to take it with me, and I'm glad I did, as it proved to be useful there.

We headed to Washington Dulles International Airport and boarded Air India's newest nonstop flight to Delhi. It was tough to leave my family, but it had to be done. Kedar's escorting me was a huge help, and his presence made what could have been a wearying experience an enjoyable one. It proved to be a big bonding experience, the kind it takes two old friends to share. As has been my habit over the years, I came up with a top ten list of my observations (mostly funny). This time it was about Kedar during our trip. The list will forever be between Kedar and myself, my close friends, and folks who also know him well. But I am sure he will not mind my sharing a couple of items from it. He is a naturally a jovial person who makes little things such as an irritating passenger sitting in front of us seem hilariously funny. At one point, like the true salesman he is, Kedar delivered an enthusiastic sales pitch to the flight crew about the benefits of nature care at Nimba. Of course, he'd never even been there. I found it hilarious, and thanks to him, I received nonstop laughter therapy as we flew halfway around the globe.

If Kedar didn't really know what Nimba was about, I can't say that I knew what to expect there either. Not only was Nimba new, neither one of us had ever been to the state of Gujarat. I had been willing to give it a try because it combined Western and Eastern approaches to healing at an affordable cost. I had spoken with Dr. Shyam and felt he understood my concerns about not abandoning physical therapy, even as I explored yoga, energy healing, and other holistic healing practices. Beyond that, I wasn't sure how I would react to what the facility could do for me. I thought, "I have nothing to lose." My doctors back in the States had similar thoughts as well.

We arrived in Delhi after a comfortable sixteen-hour flight. Even though it was quite long, I managed it okay. Monica's cousin Nikhil, who works at the airport, was there to offer help. My father-in-law, a gentle and lovable person, was also there to lend support. When we arrived in the transit area of the brand-new airport, Kedar and I, who are both big cricket fans, were happy to spot Virat Kohli, the captain of the Indian cricket team. From there, we flew to Ahmedabad, the closest big city to Mehsana, the town where Nimba is located. I was surprised when the wheel-chair attendant who picked me up outside the plane at the airport took me down a side road to the terminal a quarter of a mile away instead of to the shuttle bus. Kedar rode the bus and watched me as I was being pushed in my chair. I saw him on the bus, and we thought it was amusing, but I did make excellent time to the terminal. Nimba had a car and driver waiting for us. I asked Kedar to text "The Eagle has landed" to family and friends back home. Kedar kept up the laughter therapy as we rode to our destination. The ride to Nimba, about one hour from the airport, was quite bumpy as the highway had many potholes due to recent monsoons.

When we arrived at Nimba, it was dark. The gated campus looked isolated, and we suddenly were not sure about whether it had been the right decision to come. But as we entered, I was struck by its pristine landscaping and its graceful 200-acre campus. My twenty-four-hour aide, Vinubhai, whom my father-in-law had hired from a local Ahmedabad hospital, was there to greet us. He was a small, thin man with a lot of experience as a caregiver. He reminded me of my home aide, Pearl, back in Virginia.

Folks from Gujarat add a suffix to men's and women's names: *bhai*, meaning "brother," or *ben*, meaning "sister." It took me a while to get used to using that suffix. I did that mostly for folks who were from Gujarat.

After checking in at the front desk, I was taken in a golf cart to my room in one of the guest bungalows. My quarters were clean and fully equipped. It was too soon for me to know if I would be comfortable, though. I noted how peaceful and quiet the campus was. Being an urban person, I was used to a certain level of noise. I hoped things would not be *too* quiet!

I was glad that I had Kedar for company at the beginning of my stay. Vinubhai also shared the room with us. He slept on a mattress on the floor of my room. Although I needed it, it was a major adjustment for me to have an aide sharing my room and be there with me constantly.

Kedar kept me laughing while he was there. He always had a funny comment to make about something or other, such as the portion-controlled vegetarian food, having a twenty-four-hour aide, the room, everything. I managed to talk him into having massage treatments, even though I knew he did not like massages—but he did enjoy it. Together, we started to make friends with the Nimba residents, like Poonam, a lively and kind lady who made us feel welcome. She gave us insight into the workings of Nimba. I think everyone who met Kedar was sorry to see him leave five days later, as he bonded quite well with the residents and staff, as well as with Vinubhai. Before he left to visit with his parents in Mumbai, he asked me, "How can you stay here for three weeks?" He wondered about this, not because the facilities weren't nice, but because Nimba was very quiet, isolated, and far away from my family. I wondered about that myself—the lifestyle was so different from what I was used to. I guessed I was going to find out.

The process started with my meeting with Dr. Shyam, a stocky, intelligent, and caring person. As Nimba's chief medical officer, he was responsible for my initial evaluation and care. He began by taking my pulse, a standard procedure in traditional Indian Ayurvedic medicine, but completely different from what a Western doctor would do. A review of my medical records told him how serious my case was. I could tell he wanted me to succeed in getting well. He said he was optimistic the holistic treatments, including Ayurvedic medicine, would help me more than Western medicine had. He was more optimistic than I was. Still, I was willing to try what he recommended, despite my fear that I would remain stuck at same recovery level. I shared my feelings with him and his wife, Dr. Deepti, who was also a resident doctor on staff and did energy healing therapies with me. They told me to be patient; there was no magic pill that would restore me to the life I'd known before my stroke, but holistic treatments would certainly help. Dr. Shyam was confident that my recovery level would improve by the time I left.

It took me about a week to settle into a daily routine at Nimba. Things usually went like this:

- An early wake-up between 5:30 a.m. and 6:00 a.m. Vinubhai would get breakfast and herbal tea for me. (I was going without coffee. A big change!)
- One to two hours of physical therapy in the gym.
- Sixty to ninety minutes of Ayurvedic massage.
- Back to my bungalow, shave and bathe, sitting on a plastic chair (with the help of Vinubhai).
- Lunch in the dining hall or in my bungalow.
- An afternoon nap. (My doctors had highly advised that I take naps to rest my brain.)
- One hour of yoga, energy healing, nature therapy, or raga music therapy.
- Thirty-minute Ayurvedic massage.
- Back to my bungalow for a shower.
- Dinner in the dining hall around 6:00 p.m.
- Back to my bungalow. Spend time exchanging emails and texts with family and friends.
- Lights out at 8:00 p.m.

Although Vinubhai was quite helpful, and I am truly grateful to him, it was difficult to have someone else help me with my daily chores. I was just not used to it—not just sharing a room and having someone near me twenty-four-hours a day, but having someone to do very personal chores for me. Vinubhai was like my shadow. That was his job.

Some of Vinubhai's daily tasks included:

- Squeezing toothpaste onto my toothbrush.

- Shaving me.

- Bathing me while I sat in a chair.

- Later, when I was able to stand while taking a shower, he would stand outside the shower in case I needed anything, then help me walk across the bathroom because the floor was slippery. Then he would dry me, pick clothes, and dress me.

- Apply gel to and comb my hair.

- Trim my nails when required.

- Push me in the transporter or wheelchair to all my treatments and to the dining hall.

- Walk with me when I transitioned to a cane.

Besides Ayurvedic treatments and practices, massages were completely new to me. Based upon the ancient Indian principles of Ayurveda ("the science of life"), they seek to create a balance between mind, body, and spirit. Instead of focusing purely on the symptoms of illness, the treatment addresses root causes in a holistic way. Essential oils are a key part of Ayurvedic massage. I had no idea that different Ayurvedic massages used different oils. Dr. Shyam was a great believer in the healing power of oils. I thought he was a little obsessed with them, but I didn't see any harm in trying.

Imocha was one of my favorite massage therapists. He was a skillful guy from the far northeastern Indian state of Manipur. Every massage person was from a different region of India, of different religion or caste—so were the other staff and guests.

The caste system in India has been prevalent for centuries, and divides the Hindu society into social hierarchical groups based on what a person does and what their duties are. It's organized primarily into four groups: Brahmins (teachers and priests), Kshatriyas (warriors), Vaishyas (traders), and Shudras (laborers). Beyond the four main groups, there are about 3,000 or so other castes. One of them are the Dalits (untouchables) who do work no one else wants to do like cleaning toilets or attending bodies at funerals and are at the bottom of this rigid social hierarchy. The caste system is quite prejudicial and discriminatory. Although discrimination based on caste is banned by the constitution, and many people like me don't subscribe to this highly unfair and discriminatory system, unfortunately it is still entrenched in the culture as it's been around since 1500 BC with harmful social consequences.

I was seeing "unity in diversity" in action at Nimba. I had heard this phrase as a child growing up in India. I didn't really know what it meant then, but I definitely do now. When I was growing up, I had never noticed or cared what ethnicity, religion, or caste people were. To me, everyone I met were fellow Indians. I also fondly remember some discussions with my late father on how diverse India was. He used to call our nation "the United States of India." How true that is.

Over the course of my stay at Nimba, the masseurs used a variety of treatments prescribed by Dr. Shyam. One was abhyangam, a massage that uses warm herb-infused oils to help balance the body's doshas. The five elements of space, air, fire, water, and earth combine to create three mind-body principles called doshas in Ayurveda. Each person inherits a unique mix of three doshas, where one is usually dominant. Abhyangam works with these to maintain physical and emotional health. Shirodhara, a therapy involving the pouring of warm oil over the forehead, was also used by the masseurs.

Yoga was another component in my wellness program. At our first consultation, I told Dr. Shyam that I had never done yoga before and didn't think I could do it now, as my physical state didn't allow for all those intense exercises and stretching. He told me that yoga was an entire system of practices that also included breathing exercises and energy healing, not just tough physical exercises and poses. Boy was I glad to hear this, as I had always thought yoga involved only difficult exercises.

I experienced this in my work with Sagar, my yoga teacher at Nimba. He instructed me in meditation, another thing that was new to me. Meditation exercises improved my sense of well-being; I've continued to do them ever since. My discussions with Sagar helped me feel better. I felt the same as I had in my sessions with Dr. Susan, my highly trained and experienced clinical psychologist back in Virginia.

Sometimes the yoga sessions were supplemented with raga music therapy. According to Wikipedia, "A raga is a melodic framework for improvisation akin to a melodic mode in Indian classical music. While the raga is a remarkable and central feature of the classical music tradition, it has no direct translation to concepts in the classical European music tradition." I had listened to this kind of traditional Indian music before, but only for fun, as my father was a huge fan. Here, I sat for half an hour or so, listening to raga on headphones as therapy. It was relaxing—a nice change from the constant exposure to cable news I was used to in the States!

I also went to gym daily and worked with Dr. Haresh, my physical therapist. He was a young, slim man who had a PhD in physical therapy. For the entire time I was there, Dr. Haresh diligently helped with daily physical therapy sessions. As a corporate businessman who is always focused on improving things, I could not help but compare the physical therapy I had done at the Inova facilities in the States with the physical therapy I was doing at Nimba. It was quite similar, with some minor differences in terminology and practices.

The entire Nimba program started to yield significant results for me. Very quickly, the treatments helped with my ongoing recovery. The different holistic treatments were good, but the Ayurvedic massages using different oils were the most effective in increasing the strength of my weak left side. Just one week of massages and physical therapy had made my left side stronger, enabling me to transition from a walker to a cane. My first walk to the dining hall, using a cane—covering about a quarter mile—was a major triumph. It really felt great not to have to use a walker for the first time in the seven months since the surgery. I recognized this was also the result of going through a lot of hard therapy sessions back in the States.

Early on, I had regained some balance and coordination without any assistance. My coordination continued to improve, my uncontrolled or repetitive eye movements reduced significantly, I was able to read and focus better, my speech cleared significantly, and the frequency of my headaches abated. I was eating and performing other fine motor tasks without much difficulty, like some typing and using a mobile phone. I was becoming fitter and started to lose weight as well. By the end of my stay, I was able to perform most daily activities and was feeling psychologically confident. I lost thirty pounds (13.7 kg), and my blood pressure averaged 125/86.

In spite of these improvements, I continued to deal with dizziness, grogginess, eye dryness, some loss of balance, and other chronic symptoms. I was able to read newspaper headlines and subheadlines, but smaller type was a challenge. Dr. Shyam gave me Ayurvedic medication for the dizziness and problems with balance and special drops for eye dryness, but there was no immediate cure.

I sometimes wondered how far these treatments could take me. I had brought a Western attitude toward medicine when I came to Nimba: I expected results right away. If you have a headache, you take a pill for it, and you feel better.

Ayurvedic medicine has a different, more holistic, long-term, and prevention-based approach. Related to this is the idea of destiny and acceptance. "It is what it is" became my new mantra. It helped me deal with minor irritations like a defective room-key card or a burst pipe in my bathroom. Patience was still a challenge.

I felt lonely and isolated. I was 8,000 miles away from my family and several hundred miles away from my mom and sister in Mumbai. For the first three or four days, I was on digital detox and had no Wi-Fi access, which made me feel even more cut off from the rest of the world. Once I got back online, thanks to a Wi-Fi gadget called a dongle, I could check in with friends and family using WhatsApp. I started to talk with my mom and sister about coming to visit me from Mumbai. I did the same thing with my father-in-law in Delhi. But really, I was counting down until my planned departure date.

As the date approached, I had to acknowledge that Nimba's holistic program was helping me, and I began to consider staying longer. Dr. Shyam was confident that my recovery levels would improve if I stayed longer. Although I was ready to go back home as planned, I extended my stay by two more weeks. Dr. Deepti could sense my anxiety during our energy healing sessions. But whatever my doubts, I knew staying longer was the right thing to do.

I was still counting the days until I could go back home. The fact that Sunita, my mom, and brother-in-law Dhananjay were coming for a visit during Diwali, the Hindu festival of lights, made the wait a little easier. When they arrived, Dr. Shyam gave them evaluations and recommended treatments to improve their own health. They were not that keen on this, since they felt they had come primarily to give me company and help. But since they were there, I insisted they give the treatments a try.

> With Dr. Shyam's permission to go off-campus for sightseeing, Sunita, Mom, and I took a trip to the Sun Temple in Modhera, an hour's drive from Nimba. This historical architectural marvel with its amazing carvings was stunning. It is one of the famous sun temples in India, like the world-famous Konark in the eastern state of Odisha. We had heard of the world-famous Konark but had no idea about Modhera—it was truly magnificent.

The Nimba staff also included us in on a Diwali program called *Sneh Milan* ("love get-together"), during which, to everyone's delight, my mom sang a few songs in our native tongue of Marathi. We showed our thanks by giving the staff cash gifts for Diwali, much as we give service providers gifts for the holidays back in the US. It is not that common in India for patients and staff to share entertainment together, so this was a special event.

After spending Diwali with me, Sunita, Dhananjay, and my mom went back to Mumbai. I missed them but continued with my therapies and rehab routine.

I was hoping my father-in-law would also visit me from Delhi and undergo various treatments for his ailments, as recommended by Dr. Shyam, but he could not leave Delhi, so I coordinated a phone consult with Dr. Shyam for him.

I appreciated being made to feel welcome at Nimba, but still needed to keep a certain distance. The guests had planned many activities to keep them entertained, including nights of Antakshari (a competition where each contestant sings the first verse of a Bollywood song that begins with the consonant upon which the previous contestant's song selection ended), Housie (a bingo-like game), and screened movies. As much as I appreciated the thought behind these invitations, I politely declined some of them. Although I still feel very connected to my heritage, having been away from my native country almost thirty years, I was not keen on these activities. I felt happier being by myself than taking part in activities, with all due respect to those guests who were excited to participate.

That said, I didn't want them to feel I was a snob declining every social activity they planned. I did enjoy being included in birthday celebrations. I distinctly remember the guests had made a birthday cake to celebrate Dr. Deepti's birthday. We took an excursion to nearby Shankus Waterpark for Navratri, another Hindu festival that celebrates the triumph of good over evil. We enjoyed *garba*, a Navratri dance popular all over India but especially a sight to behold in Gujarat. We also visited the adjoining farm where Nimba grows the organic vegetables it cooked.

In October, many at Nimba asked me, "What's going on in the US?" when they heard the sad news about the Las Vegas shooting and the vehicle ramming attack in New York City. Folks there were just not able to comprehend why there is so much violence in the US and why someone would kill so many innocent people. Over the years, I have passionately defended many things about the US, but I could not defend those. I had no answers.

I had achieved some real milestones in my recovery. I noted the changes in my health and lifestyle:

- No coffee, only herbal tea.

- First time not using a walker.

- First time standing under the shower seven months after surgery and not having to sit on a stool or chair, although still under Vinubhai's watchful eyes—an accomplishment!

- Climbing stairs in the therapy center using one arm and a cane.

- Going outside the Nimba campus for Navratri festivities at Shankus Waterpark after three full weeks of staying on campus. It felt liberating just to be outside Nimba and see other people.

Still, I was more than ready to go home to Virginia to be with my family. I felt this way even though I was right there in the country I grew up in and closer to Mumbai where my mom and sister were. Somebody asked me, "Aren't you home?" But home was where my heart was—back in Virginia where Monica, Jai, Arjun, and my friends were. It's quite interesting: while in the US, I had always told my friends, "The DC area is like home away from home for me." Now the DC area was indeed my home. Whatever way I was going to live the rest of my life, I was meant to live it in the United States. Although I already knew this, I fully realized it after coming to Nimba.

There were people who cared about me who saw things differently. Although they knew how isolating it was for me, Monica, my mom, and my mother-in-law had all separately and gently suggested that I extend my stay a second time, as I was benefiting from the "recovery boost."

> Typically, the first year after surgery is when one gets maximum benefits, and the Nimba treatments were helping a lot.

Yet I felt that I would slide into depression if I didn't go home. In the end, however, I listened to their suggestion and grudgingly agreed to stay on for four more weeks. It was a hard decision, but I had to do it, and a new countdown began.

Of course, I wasn't the only one at Nimba experiencing loneliness and sadness. Behind every smiling face, I saw there were ongoing struggles and sorrows. Some of the residents were recovering from spinal cord surgery or any number of other serious ailments. Others were being treated for irritable bowel syndrome (IBS) or alcoholism. One family I met had come to find peace after the loss of their daughter. Some came just for rejuvenating their mind and body. Some were open about what they were going through, others not. But what brought all of them there was a desire to recover and heal. Although I continued to ask myself, "Why me?" I also began to realize that other people had many problems too. You need to take care of yourself and have a positive attitude, even if you are dealing with heartaches and tragedies.

Over time, I became friendly with some of the people I saw each day, staff and guests alike. Like the staff, most of the guests came from various parts of India, though quite a few were from overseas. The staff continued to make me feel part of the Nimba community. I was a bit unusual. Folks normally came there for a week or less. By the time I left, I had been there two and a half months and had met just about everyone who worked there, including the center's owner, Babubhai Bokadia, his son Jayant, who managed Nimba, and Mr. Bhandari, who was on the Nimba board. It was nice of Babubhai to stop by the bungalow one time to see me. I still joke with my family that I am a legend at Nimba. Being a corporate type, I offered "process improvement" ideas and suggestions to make Nimba better to whomever was willing to listen. My business training and experience have taught me that most of the challenges faced by organizations are process related and typically not "people" related. I had seen this again and again throughout many global companies I worked and consulted with, and Nimba was no different. I also saw some business opportunity for Grant Thornton in India and connected with the right folks back at the mother ship in the States. I guess you cannot take the businessperson out of me, stroke or no stroke.

It felt good to spend time with Dr. Shyam and Dr. Deepti outside of Nimba at Café Coffee Day, a popular Indian coffee chain like Starbucks. I appreciated how Mr. Saniyal, the general manager, made sure I had a Wi-Fi connection in my bungalow. He also helped me get a new aide when I parted company with Vinubhai. Anaru was not a twenty-four-hour aide and did not share my room, which made things much more comfortable for me.

None of this could cure my homesickness. I especially felt it on the day I would have flown back had I not extended my stay. On October 31, I also noted that Arjun would be wearing a costume for Halloween back home. Those thoughts made me miss my family even more intensely. I mailed letters to say hello to the good folks at Inova Mount Vernon and Inova Fairfax hospitals. I started making a list of things to take back with me, such as Ayurvedic medicines and oils prescribed by Dr. Shyam, Ayurvedic medicines for Monica, and recipes of some of the food I liked in the Nimba dining hall. I was so ready to head back home. After recovering from a brief case of Delhi belly, a common digestive disorder among visitors to India, I got ready for Sunita's second visit.

This time, we did a couple of meditation sessions with Sagar as well as a hydra walk through warm, then cold water over pebbles. I was feeling strong enough to take a trip to visit Sabarmati Ashram, one of Mahatma Gandhi's residences and a famous Ahmedabad tourist attraction. One evening, we both went to the farm next door when Nimba owners and management offered a customer meet. Sunita's love and support helped to ease my loneliness at a crucial time.

One weekend, Sunita took me to Zydus Hospital in Ahmedabad, a state-of-the-art medical facility, for an evaluation with Dr. Arvind Sharma, one of the region's top neurologists. Another guest at Nimba had recommended him, and I was lucky that he managed to secure an appointment for me. After examining me and checking my vision, Dr. Sharma told me he approved of the treatment I had been receiving in the States and was happy to hear about my rehab routine at Nimba. It felt good to get confirmation that I was on the right track to recovery. Being a true networker, later on I connected Dr. Sharma with Dr. Shyam.

My regimen of treatments continued, and I was regaining my ability to do some everyday tasks. The bills I received at Nimba seemed a bit confusing; I asked for more information and managed to reconcile them. I was a details-oriented person before my stroke, so I took this as a sign that I was making progress.

Thanksgiving Day was another reminder of how much I missed my family and the things we did on holidays. It also meant that my departure was less than a week away. I was starting to wind down my treatments and get ready for the long trip home. My mom came by to see me for a second visit, and Sunita went back to Mumbai.

As much as I looked forward to going home, it was still a little tough for me to leave the kind folks I'd met at Nimba who had become my family. During the last week, I was able to walk a little in the carpeted yoga hall without a cane, under the watchful eyes of Dr. Haresh. This was a big win for me. Two days before I left, I had my final appointment with Dr. Shyam.

I thanked him profusely, and we reflected on the progress I had made and what I should do after I returned to the States. The day before I left, my mom and I had lunch with the staff in their dining hall. We distributed Indian sweets to show how much we appreciated the care they'd given me. Dr. Shyam and Dr. Deepti took my mom and me, along with Dr. Haresh, to Café Coffee Day for a final get-together. We bought items for ourselves at the Nimba gift shop along with gifts for my friends and family in the US. It seemed I was catching a cold, and Imocha came to my room to give me a head massage and apply an Ayurvedic balm. He knew how much I looked forward to returning home and wanted to help me feel better, as I was worried that I might not be able to travel. I knew I was being taken good care of right up to the end of my stay.

In summing up my stay at Nimba, Dr. Shyam provided me with a report on the progress I'd made. Not that I fully understood what these holistic treatments were, but he gave me a high-level overview of each treatment, which I have included in appendix B. Nimba no doubt had helped me get both physically stronger and become emotionally calm and relaxed.

Finally, the day of my departure arrived. That morning, I made a point to visit the therapy building and took selfies with the staff who had taken such awesome care of me. Anaru accompanied us to the airport. It was tough for me to say good-bye to Mom, who was headed back to Mumbai. I then met up with Dhananjay, who had flown in from Mumbai to fly with me to Delhi and on to Washington. I was truly grateful and thankful for where I was in terms of my recovery and the progress I'd made during my stay at Nimba and was glad I had come here.

I can honestly say that not any single treatment was decisive in advancing my recovery. What I can say is that *all* of what I did there was helpful. I was determined to continue moving forward with my new normal. Dhananjay and I began our trek back to DC.

• • •

"Nature has the healing power, only we require will power."

—JAYANT BOKADIA, CEO of Nimba

Health Recovery Level

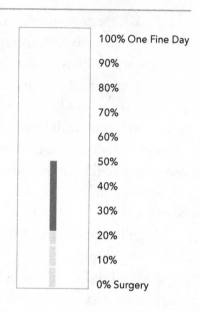

100% One Fine Day

90%

80%

70%

60%

50%

40%

30%

20%

10%

0% Surgery

SAMEERISM

- There is no magic pill or potion, whether in Western or Eastern medicine, which offers a total cure. Physical, mental rehab and grit is the only way to move forward.

- Behind every smiling face is some kind of sorrow or adversity. Never assume anything. Everyone is fighting some kind of battle. Help others. Be kind and compassionate toward others.

CHAPTER 5

Craving Stability

"Happiness is a conscious choice, not an automatic response."

MILDRED BARTHEL

Dhananjay and I had a delicious dinner at the Delhi airport lounge before boarding our long flight back to the States. Our Air India flight was comfortable, and I was glad it was a nonstop straight into Dulles and not connecting through Europe or the Middle East. The flight also allowed me to bond with Dhananjay—no sister, no mom, and no work for him—just two brothers-in-law hanging out. The flight crew was kind and helpful and took excellent care of us. They were Mumbai-based, so we had good conversations with them about the place I grew up. One can debate Air India flight service and facilities, but nobody can debate the awesome food they serve. Dhananjay was amazed when the crew said they knew some of my college friends who worked as cabin crew with the airline as well. I recommended some good places they could go to eat in the DC area before their return flight. When we arrived at Washington Dulles, they gave me a small bottle of champagne. It pays to be friendly!

There were huge lines to get through immigration—something that always used to get me riled up. Waiting in a wheelchair was tedious, but I remained calm. My "it is what it is" mantra was taking hold. These annoyances couldn't dispel the happiness I felt at arriving back home.

I was exhausted but happy with the progress I'd made. The flight had left me with a bad case of jet lag, so I slept a lot for the first five days back. I avoided phone calls and exchanged texts only with friends. From the moment I boarded the flight to India with Kedar to the moment I arrived back home with Dhananjay, I had been shown love, friendship, and compassion, just like I had experienced at home since my stroke. As I'd done for Kedar, I did my "top ten" list of observations about Dhananjay for our trip back. I was grateful beyond words for what loved ones and newly made friends had done for me. This was a key part of my healing. Dhananjay left a few days later to return to Mumbai. Now I was ready to get back to my new normal with my family.

I was working to heal my mind and spirit as well as my body, and my regimen now consisted of a combination of Western and Eastern medicine, care, and practices. I took what I'd learned at Nimba and continued to use Ayurvedic medicines and oils and ate mostly vegetarian meals. Meditation became part of my regular routine.

Beyond specific treatments and therapies, the holistic approach to health and life itself influenced me in lasting ways, without overdoing it, though. I also continued with the daily journaling habit I'd begun at Nimba, along with writing down three things I was proud of and grateful for every day. Before I started doing this, I had been a big to-do list person but never documented my feelings on paper. I was surprised by how cathartic this simple practice was. To date, I continue to do it.

I am very grateful to be the beneficiary of both Western and Eastern systems of medicine and care. But I don't believe one system is better than the other. Just as some people are overly dependent on Western medicine, there are people who only use alternate medicines, practices, and care, and shun cutting-edge medical innovations and technology. I am absolutely convinced that you need both in balance. Also, because I'm Indian, some people, both in India and in the States, assumed that I am in total support of Eastern medicine and care, especially Ayurveda. Nobody said so specifically, but I could sense it. I have to be honest: Ayurveda is not the answer to all the ills, as many folks believe, nor is Western medicine and technology. You need both. They complement one another well. I am living proof.

Upon my return, I also resumed visits with my neurologist, Dr. Manem, and went to my internist, Dr. Rachel, for a blood test. I was happy with the results and sent them on to Dr. Shyam, since I wanted to keep him informed about my progress. I got evaluated at Inova Fairfax Hospital for further physical and occupational therapy. I also started seeing my clinical psychologist, Dr. Susan, again. I shared with her what I'd done at Nimba and what I planned to do now that I was back home. She didn't offer her opinions or judge me in any way. She listened and allowed me to confide in her. I'd never done that with anyone before.

On days I was not doing therapy, I would spend an hour or so doing Nimba exercises at home, including visual exercises, and pranayam, closing one nostril and taking deep breaths—a common breathing technique in yoga. You can't practice it for long; ten minutes feels like running twenty minutes on a treadmill. Bhramari, another yoga technique I practiced, involves putting your fingers in your ears and making a bee-like humming sound; the vibrations clear your head. Bhramari offers long-term benefits rather than big effects right away. I also chanted the mantra "om," using different frequencies. All this was in addition to regular exercises like sit-ups, push-ups, leg raises, and so forth. Dr. Shyam also gave me a high-level overview of these exercises, which I have included in appendix D. The meditation techniques I had learned at Nimba were not easy to do but had many benefits. I really wanted Sagar to continue the guided meditation sessions, but now he was 8,000 miles away. Technically, I could do it by myself (self-meditation) or use an app or You-Tube video for guided meditation. But there was something special about Sagar's sessions; he had a calm demeanor and, even though he talked about life philosophies and universe-related things, he had a practical side to his guidance, which was appealing to this analytical and practical person. The sessions definitely had helped me to become calmer and more relaxed. I had always leveraged technology to help me with my tasks at work, so I asked Sagar if he was comfortable doing meditation sessions via Skype or WhatsApp. He said he had never done remote guided sessions that way, but gave his nod for us to try. Each week, I did a remote guided meditation session with him for thirty to forty-five minutes. A practice I still continue.

At Nimba, the meditation and holistic treatments had given me a stronger ability to accept destiny and relinquish the need for control. Back home, that process continued. I realized I had to accept a situation the way it is, not the way I might want it to be. My "it is what it is" mantra continued to develop further. I used to get angry over little things, like paying bills or dealing with bad equipment. Now I was becoming more patient and accepting while learning to look for realistic solutions to everyday problems. The mantra "it is what it is" applies to so many things. It can be a difficult message to follow, but it has gotten easier over time.

For many years, I had been part of a reactive and competitive business world. In business, generally, you don't look calmly at a situation and acknowledge how the other party sees things. Being empathetic is just not part of the business culture. Because of my stroke, I was beginning to take a very different view of life. I was becoming calmer and more compassionate and empathetic. When I return to regular work in the future, it will be interesting to see what my reaction will be. Maybe my sense of acceptance will flow into the business world.

The Christmas and holiday season was approaching fast. Monica and I wanted our boys to have a break; they had gone through a lot over the past ten months. We got them Amtrak tickets to go visit Kedar and Vrinda and their girls, who they adored, in New Jersey. Friends and colleagues checked in with me. It especially felt good to speak with my boss, Dave. My friend Sal stopped by to install a TV in the basement, something I knew Arjun would appreciate. It was comforting to know so many were willing to pitch in and help. I was particularly touched that a group of friends helped to paint Arjun's room in Harry Potter–themed colors and patterns. We knew this would mean a lot to him. Britt, Ron's girlfriend and also our friend who is a professional event planner, took the lead and handled all the details. She chose the paint, planned out the room décor, and got everybody organized. It was a big job to finish, but Britt, Ron, Kyran, Lydia, Chandu, and Emanuele got it done brilliantly.

We were incredibly grateful to everyone who helped make it happen. "This is our real America!" That's how I felt when I thought about acts of kindness like this. We are friends, regardless of ethnicity, nationality, residential status, or economic stratum. The United States is a true melting pot, no matter what anyone says.

Jai was back home for the holidays. I was glad to see that he was finding his way at his university. On his own, he had changed his major. I could see his happiness when he showed me his new course curriculum. I was proud that he had made these decisions on his own.

Meanwhile, Arjun let us know that he wanted a hover-board for Christmas. Monica had valid concerns about their safety, so he did some research and then gave me some discussion points in their favor. He knew I was relatively easy to convince. He said, "Dad, use these to convince mom." I was impressed with his ability to construct an argument based upon data and information. I said to myself, "This is a future businessperson in action! Young Arjun is really selling the idea of a hoverboard!" He won the argument fair and square and received the gift he wanted. I am convinced he can use those skills in the future.

It was important to me to spend more time with Arjun. There was one special day while Monica was at a grocery store when I was home with him alone for the first time after my stroke. I don't recall what we talked about. It didn't matter. The important thing was that the two of us could share time together. We also went out to the Olive Garden with his friend Chloe—my first visit to a restaurant in ten months. It made me happy because I could go with Arjun to one of his favorite restaurants.

My time back home was filled with meaningful moments with my family and friends. Among them were the walks I took around our neighborhood with Monica and our friend Kyran. Being able to walk outside with a cane was a milestone. I could only cover about a half a mile, but that didn't make it any less important. Part of the path we took covered a stretch of road where I had taught Jai and Arjun to ride bicycles. During our walk, that was the kind of thing I could share with Kyran, an understanding guy who is very family oriented. Years earlier, I had run behind my sons as they learned to ride bikes; now, I could barely walk. Before, I would have thought, "Why am I so unlucky?" Now, I had slowly started to accept life as it is. Here I was, out on the road, moving forward.

With the end of the year approaching, I reached another turning point in my recovery. I knew that the coming winter, always a difficult time in the Northeast, even for the able-bodied, would keep me stuck at home. I would have to impose upon Monica to help me get to my medical and therapy appointments. Both Monica and my mom gently suggested that I return to India for more rehab. Although Nimba was nice, and the program there had been hugely beneficial for me, there was no way I could return to a far-off place like that again. I had asked Dr. Shyam before I returned home whether staying beyond November would be helpful. Although Nimba would have continued to help me rehab, the rate of improvement would not be as high as it was in September. In business, we call that diminishing returns. Also, it was obvious that I was lonely and missed my family and friends, having been away from them for almost three months. The cost of staying outweighed the benefits of staying longer. Going back home from Nimba at the end of November had made total sense. Going there again did not.

I could now walk with a cane and did not need a wheelchair or a walker. So this time, I could stay at my sister's high-rise apartment. Sunita and Dhananjay generously agreed to take me into their home in Mumbai. In addition to the favorable climate, the shift would bring several other advantages: plentiful and affordable home therapists, affordable drivers and domestic help, and of course the company of my sister and mother and the familiarity of the neighborhood where I grew up. My mother would be turning seventy-five in February, which gave me another reason to be in my hometown. Anil graciously agreed to fly with me to Mumbai. Monica and my mom both said, "At a minimum, you will miss the harsh DC winter." That clinched the deal.

Once I decided to return to Mumbai, we kept busy taking care of last-minute details. There were discussions about our finances, obtaining my MRI, CAT scans, and blood reports from Inova Fairfax Hospital and Dr. Rachel, and scheduling follow-up visits with Dr. Vyas. I also did certain tasks as I had before my stroke: paying bills, connecting friends who would benefit professionally, planning my trip with the travel agent and insisting that he book my tickets on any Star Alliance flights to maximize loyalty points. These activities and this analytical behavior in particular were very much *me*. I was back—almost. My new normal was slowly taking shape.

We also had to make a decision about our second car. I had purchased an expensive two-door Audi A5 two years earlier. Now it was sitting in the driveway idle, and it didn't make sense to keep it any longer. Jai and Arjun loved the car as much as I did, but the cost of maintaining it was too high. Even though it was hard for me and the boys, it made sense to sell it.

Monica also started figuring out what kind of rehab I'd need, and Sunita began researching caregivers who could visit me in her home. I reached out to my own friends and contacts, Dr. Anant Joshi, for example, a US-trained pioneer of sports medicine in India and founder of Sportsmed Mumbai (a top integrated sports medicine facility), whom I knew from my childhood days as a competitive badminton player. Even though he was quite my senior, I had called him Antya, as do many of his friends. I contacted another friend named Amod, who is a doctor in Abu Dhabi, and asked him for a recommendation for a neurologist. He recommended Dr. Satish Khadilkar, the head of neurology at Bombay Hospital. This would turn out to be a critically helpful recommendation.

Anil and Aparna came to Virginia a few days before we were to leave. It was tough to say good-bye to my family again, as I knew I would be gone for at least a few months on this second trip to India, which I'd begun to think of as Offshore Rehab 2.0. But it had to be done.

• • •

"Success is how high you bounce when you hit bottom."

—GEORGE S. PATTON

Health Recovery Level

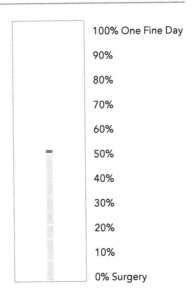

100% One Fine Day

90%

80%

70%

60%

50%

40%

30%

20%

10%

0% Surgery

SAMEERISM • One's healing is enhanced when people from different backgrounds and from around the world gather to help you (the global village). Only by working across borders and in cooperation with one another can we achieve the full extent of our human abilities.

CHAPTER 6

In Search of a Magic Pill —Part Deux

"If the plan doesn't work, change the plan, but never the goal."

UNKNOWN

My friend Kyran's sister-in-law, Stella, who worked for United Airlines, put in a good word on my behalf with the crew that would be taking us to India that night. I'd never even met her! Not that I didn't think the crew would take good care of me, but her assistance greatly reduced my anxiety about the long voyage.

Anil's company was also a tremendous help. During the flight, we could not stop thinking about our train trip to the Badminton Nationals in 1985. The train was the Jammu Tavi Express, named after the largest railway station in Jammu and Kashmir, and we had both traveled in coach class. We passed the time on the long flight comparing the two different journeys and laughing about the differences now that we were both nearing the fifty-year mark and could afford to surround ourselves with the comforts and luxury of business class. Later, as I had done for Kedar and Dhananjay for the Nimba trips, I came up with my "top ten" list for Anil. Like Kedar's and Dhananjay's lists, Anil's will forever be between us and my close friends who also know Anil well. I am sure he will also not mind my sharing something from it. Beyond the great conversation and memories, Anil held my hand and helped me get to the bathroom on the flight, accidentally providing a funny memory when we discovered the power outlet on his seat didn't work. Those who know Anil will recognize that such things happen to him all the time.

Thanks to Stella, the crew took extra care of us. I remember some of them, like Eugene and Francine. They were total strangers but showed us such kindness. I know some will say that it was their job, but to do their jobs in such a compassionate way is something special. One of them brought a smile to my face when she walked by and noted Anil curled up in his seat, sleeping peacefully. "Oh, let the sleeping beauty sleep," she said. "I will bring his meal later."

After a long sixteen-hour nonstop but comfortable flight, we landed in Mumbai safely. Sunita and Dhananjay greeted us, and Offshore Rehab 2.0 was officially underway. During the ride home, I remember teasing Sunita's driver, Vikas, who had put on some weight since the last time I'd seen him in 2015. He had recently been married. The exchange helped me to feel right at home back in India.

Sunita and Dhananjay live in a fantastic high-rise in the Prabhadevi area of midtown Mumbai, directly opposite from the famous Shree Siddhivinayak Temple, a Lord Ganesha temple popular with many. Although I was with my loving sister and brother-in-law, it was definitely odd to be in someone else's house, and strange to know I was going to be there until April. It's not easy to have someone in your house for so much time, even if it's your brother and there is domestic help. I am forever indebted to Sunita and Dhananjay.

Sunita gave me the guest room in her apartment. In the guest bathroom, she had installed handrails, which I needed and were much appreciated. Everything else was just perfect.

Offshore Rehab 2.0

After a few days of getting over my jet lag, I made an appointment to see Dr. Antya Joshi at Sportsmed. It was great to see him after so many years. Even though he was aging, he still was as fit and active as a thirty-year-old. He had been a sportsman when he was younger, and now was into cycling and had many bikes in his garage and biked his way to Sportsmed every day. Some people called him a "psyclepath" due to his dedication to and obsession with this low-impact sport. As he was now a famous orthopedic surgeon in India, I asked him if I should call him Antya or Dr. Joshi. He wanted me to call him Antya, as I did before.

Neither fame, fortune, or success had changed him over

the years; he was as humble and lovable as he was when he had just started the concept of sports medicine in India in the 1980s. He evaluated me and was happy with the progress of my physical rehab so far. He confirmed the recommendation for Dr. Khadilkar, the neurologist, and connected me with his friend Dr. Ali Irani, the head of the physiotherapy department at the Nanavati Hospital in the suburbs.

My care started with a visit to Dr. Khadilkar at Bombay Hospital. Sunita and Dhananjay accompanied me for the appointment, where Dr. Khadilkar evaluated me and declared his satisfaction with my progress. He is an old-school neurologist, calm and reassuring, and just a wonderful person. Because of my ongoing struggles with dizziness and balance, he ordered an MRI for me—the first one since my surgery. He wanted to rule out any possible new issues, such as a return of the bleeding. We left the hospital feeling good that an esteemed neurologist was satisfied with my progress. Now we just hoped that the MRI results would be okay and there was no new bleeding.

We were exhausted when we returned to the apartment from the hospital. Although we had a nice car and driver, just getting around in Mumbai traffic can be tiring!

I made an appointment for the MRI at the local Hinduja Hospital, relatively close to Sunita's apartment. There was a two-day wait, which gave us plenty of time to stew in anxiety. On the day of the appointment, the neuroimaging staff was highly efficient. The visit was also interesting because a patient's relative there offered me advice on how the neurosurgeon at Inova Fairfax should have performed my surgery! It was a reminder of what it meant to be back in India: we love to give free advice and opinions, even when it's not about our area of expertise. It's always well-meaning and a way we have of taking care of one another. With the MRI complete, the extra prayers started.

While we waited, we settled into our new routine. Sunita made me meals daily, beginning with healthy breakfasts including fresh fruits, different nuts, soups, and so on. She also had a cook who would come daily and whip up delicious healthy entrées from various cuisines as well as fresh roti, a type of Indian bread I especially love. What a treat that was—freshly made rotis every day! We also ordered delivery of delicious food from different local restaurants. In the first week, Sunita ordered quesadillas and brought home a menu from a place that had just opened called Menu Fresh. I took a look at the menu and told her, "I get stuff like that back in Virginia!"

"Let's try it," she said, looking dubious; it was standard fare for the States, but not typical of Mumbai. We ordered Chinese fried rice and wings, and yes, it was all delicious. It brought me a taste of home and made the world seem a little smaller. The food was simply divine, as my father-in-law would often say. Over the years, Dhananjay and I had shared a fondness for single-malt Scotch whisky, but now I could not have alcohol, so he developed a recipe for a non-alcoholic mojito that was not quite the same thing, but made me feel welcome and cared for nonetheless.

We also started the hiring process for a physical therapist who could come visit me at home. Dr. Irani at Nanavati

Hospital sent a therapist, Priyanka, who evaluated me—and I evaluated her as well. By this point, I had gained a lot of knowledge about therapies and treatments and was in a position to determine whether she had the knowledge and expertise to be my therapist; and she did indeed. Having passed the Sameer test, she started therapy sessions with me.

When the MRI results came in, we were so anxious that we tried to understand the report ourselves. It looked like it was okay, but with our limited understanding of medical terms, it was challenging to understand it, so I instantly texted it to my cousin Medha, who is a doctor in Pune. She read the report and told us it looked good and that she could see no new bleeding. Boy, was I glad to hear that! She wasn't a neurologist, though, so she said it would be good for Dr. Khadilkar to take a look and give his opinion. We saw Dr. Khadilkar a couple of days later, and he was happy to see the results. He confirmed Medha's findings, and we could see the visible relief on his face.

He approved our physical therapy plan, and I asked him about my continuing dizziness and balance issues. After eliminating other factors that might be causing it, like temperature, barometric pressure, whether or not I worked out, medications, and so on, he said he did not know if the dizziness would subside or by how much. He said, "For most people it comes down, in my experience." But since I had undergone massive surgeries on the cerebellum to remove the vascular abnormalities, he just didn't know when. At the time, I didn't know that this was to become my single biggest ongoing fight—and one I will continue to struggle with even years after the stroke. Every day I wake up and feel as if I have a half bottle of Scotch whisky running through my system. The dizziness affects all aspects of my life, and I sometimes find myself canceling appointments or other plans because of it. At the time, though, I was happy just to have confirmation that the surgery had been successful and my brain was healing.

I started my physical therapy sessions with Priyanka. She would come to the apartment two or three times a week and conduct the therapy sessions with me, then go to her full-time job at the hospital. After a couple of weeks, she found that the travel required for the house calls was too much for her, so she recommended another therapist from her hospital who lived close by. And lo and behold, the new therapist was also a Priyanka. What were the chances? The new Priyanka also passed the Sameer test and was my therapist until the end.

After working with her for a time, I hit a big milestone: I was able to get up and down the hallway by myself, cane in hand, to use the elevators to go downstairs to the gym or to the rec center. It was the first time I was independent enough to go to therapy by myself. My real goal, however, was to be able to navigate the steep slope outside the parking garage of my sister's apartment building. It was about forty-five to fifty feet long, and tackling it would require big gains in my balance and strength and coordination. But I was determined.

Besides physical therapy, my rehab routine continued to include yoga exercises and remote guided meditation sessions with Sagar. As part of his guided meditations, Sagar had made many brilliant statements, but I remember him saying in particular, "Thoughts will come and go. Emotions will come and go. They are all temporary, but awareness is permanent. Be patient, be compassionate to yourself and others."

I also began working with Harish, a trainer in the gym at the apartment complex, and I started aqua therapy in the pool downstairs, with Dinesh, the lifeguard, watching over me.

My Life Coach

One of Dhananjay's friends recommended a masseur who could come visit me at the apartment. This was how I met Nagesh, who was not only a good masseur, but also my quasi psychologist, neurologist, physical therapist, trainer, and all-around life coach—all in one. He was a kind man who had advice and suggestions for practically everything: health, wellness, technology, politics—you name it! I took his advice with a grain of salt, but I knew it was well-meaning, and I genuinely appreciated his support and his ability to make the time fly. Over the two or three months we worked together, we developed a unique bond. My sister was always curious to know what I talked about with him each time. He made some classic statements over the months, but I distinctly remember when he said, in my mother tongue Marathi, "Sir, isn't it amazing that they cracked open your skull to do the brain surgery?" I chuckled for sure. He was genuinely stunned.

While developing an aqua therapy regimen with Dinesh, I found out he was not only a lifeguard but also an excellent trainer. I joked with him that he should start selling aqua therapy services along with his swimming lessons and that he could use me as a reference. He was punctual, diligent, kind, and gentle. While we were working together in the pool, there were generally few other patrons, so it was like a private pool for me, other than the crows and pigeons who would hang around on the deck. Swimming with crows and pigeons was a unique experience indeed.

I worked hard with Dinesh and also learned about his family. He asked me questions about life in the States. He played my favorite music on the pool speakers and helped me dry myself after swimming, then helped me walk back to the elevator. Although progress was good in many areas, I continued to experience spikes in my dizziness and started to realize this was to be my new normal. Dr. Khadilkar had given me tablets to help with it, but they weren't effective, so when it happened, I'd cancel therapy sessions and just rest.

Connections and Visitors

From my mother I have inherited a tendency to talk to people and make friendly conversations very quickly. I believe that much of the progress I've made with my healing has come from the support of people around me, whether family, friends, caretakers, or just those I came across regularly. During my time in Mumbai, there were many such people. There was a father-son duo who used to come to the gym in the apartment building. The son was about my age and had been to the States a number of times, so he and I would talk regularly. The elderly father would contribute to our conversations sometimes, and one day, I invited him to come swim with me. A few days later, I was thrilled when he showed up along with his in-law visiting from Kolkata. Both father and son provided me with a lot of encouragement as I worked in the gym to get my body well again. One of the memories I have of the gym where I labored during my many physical therapy sessions with Priyanka and Harish still makes me chuckle. One day on the TV in the gym, a Bollywood song played. I knew who the actress was. Being a millennial, Priyanka knew her face, and said, "Oh, she is Shraddha Kapoor's aunt." Shraddha Kapoor was a new Bollywood star popular with young folks. I thought to myself, "Oh boy, I am getting old!" It was the young star's aunt. I guess fifty was fast approaching!

I continued to try different therapies outside my official rehab program for my ongoing dizziness and balance issues. At Sportsmed, I met an Australian osteopathic therapist named Taylor, and I did a few sessions with him. Though it didn't help much with the dizziness, I achieved some gains with my coordination and strength. Beyond that, I discovered in Taylor another fan of the NFL. He was a huge fan of the Philadelphia Eagles—the archrivals of my favorite team, the Washington Redskins! It was funny to be an Indian American sitting in Mumbai and talking to an Australian about American football. The league is indeed global! I can't help but think that our spirited exchanges also contributed to my healing. My sister had no idea what the heck we were talking about.

Sunita would occasionally consult with an astrologer named Mr. Pancholi regarding her son, Sahil, who has some medical issues. Although not a big believer herself, her attitude was *let's try it for my son*. She cautiously asked me if I wanted to consult the astrologer as well. She knew I was not a big believer in organized religion, astrology, and the like, but I agreed with her thinking: try everything! She immediately made an appointment. Typically, astrologers will look at your horoscope, which are charts based on the positions of the sun, moon, stars, and planets at the time of your birth, then interpret them and make predictions for your future. Mr. Pancholi was a kind senior citizen, and he looked at my horoscope, which my sister and mom had made for me, and gave his thoughts. I don't want to nor can I comment on whether visiting an astrologer is a thing to do, since it is a personal choice based on your beliefs. I certainly was not a big believer, but I can definitely say that talking to him felt a little bit like talking to Dr. Susan, my clinical psychologist back in Virginia.

Many folks from my childhood came to see me. I made sure to see Mr. and Mrs. M. G. Bhide, who share my last name but aren't family relations, though they are certainly like family to me. They live on the second floor of the apartment building where my mom lives and where I grew up.

Mr. Bhide was a close friend of my father's, and I grew up admiring him.

I also had visits with other local friends and from the States. My dear friends from Virginia, Lydia and her husband, Chandu, who is originally from India, stopped by to say hello. I was delighted to see them and happy to introduce them to Sunita and Dhananjay.

Dave continued to be in constant touch with me via email and phone. Dave was not only my boss but also a friend, mentor, and confidante, and I was happy to have his support. He informed me about the sad passing of our dear colleague Chris Steinhardt. He was close to Chris (in fact he had also asked Chris to interview me). I asked Monica to send flowers to his family and donate to the charity he supported. RIP Chris.

Sahil came to visit from Pune. He had lost a lot of weight since the last time I saw him in 2015; he was looking good, fit, and trim, and as handsome as ever.

My father-in-law in Delhi, whom I was close to, was in constant touch with me as well—he had been very worried about my health over the past year. I also made a point of connecting with some folks I hadn't spoken to in many years, in some cases since my childhood, such as former neighbors, my badminton coach, and my father's sister in Pune. I also befriended the staff of the apartment building and the domestic staff, who used to come to Sunita's daily. Ratika, Meena, and Uma were truly kind and compassionate. I made conversation with them whenever I could. They hesitated to speak with me as they saw me as *sahib*, a word common in the Indian Subcontinent. The word is from India's colonial past, used when talking about the British or Europeans. Now it's used when addressing people of a higher social or official status. But we treated each other with respect, and they lovingly called me *Dada*, which means "elder brother" in Marathi. Each of these connections gave me a little more strength and helped me along my way.

I heard that, back in Virginia, my friend Vinu's father had died. Although he had not been well, he seemed to have been recovering, so his passing came as a shock. Having lost my father six years earlier, I knew the pain and void his family felt. I called Vinu and told him that no matter what anyone says, it's okay to grieve.

And then, of course, there was my dear mom! On Sunita's birthday, my mom and I took her for a birthday lunch to Bombay Brasserie, her favorite restaurant. After lunch, I went to my mom's apartment for the first time during the trip. She proudly showed me the newly painted rooms.

I was thrilled and grateful to be able to attend her seventy-fifth birthday party a few days after my sister's birthday. Sunita planned a nice party for her and invited the many good folks from my mom's apartment building to her home. My mom grinned with joy that day, and I thanked God for giving me the opportunity to celebrate her special day.

Daily Diversions

Beyond my physical and social therapies, I found other ways to fill my time to keep myself occupied and mentally engaged. I ordered *tabla* (Indian drums) on the suggestion of Datta, a fit trainer in the gym who was friendly with me while I trained with Harish. I'd learned tabla as a child and found that playing again was good for my hands and brain as a sort of therapy.

I put my computer skills to work by helping Sunita with some software support, and I continued with my passion for helping people find job opportunities back in the States, using my extensive network. I find it empowering when I can help people find the right opportunities or connections. And then of course, there was television, both Indian and American programs, including a crazy Marathi soap opera called *Mazhya navryachi bayko* ("My Husband's Wife"), which would put American soap operas to shame. The storylines were so scandalous that Sunita, Dhananjay, and I were always eager to see what happened every day in each episode. We would adjust our dinnertime so that we could watch the show without interruption, and we would speculate what might happen in the episode before it started.

I also found time to read, even though it took only ten minutes or so before my eyes got tired. Anil had introduced me via email to Vijay Santanam, another stroke survivor, who'd written a book called *My Stroke of Luck*. I found it to be an encouraging read, and that's when the initial thought for *One Fine Day* began to form. Vijay was kind enough to talk with me on the phone, and I found him inspiring and motivating, just as he'd been in his book. In the meantime, Monica was writing a beautiful book called *I See You* about her experience as a caregiver at the ICU during my illness. She sent me the draft to review and I gave her my feedback, just as I'd done for all the years she'd been a writer. Once she published the book, I sent out targeted emails to friends, family, and acquaintances, requesting them to spread the word. The inspiration behind *One Fine Day* was cemented.

I settled into a regular routine of waking up early, around 5:30 a.m. or 6:00 a.m. I'd check my emails and text messages and then do an hour of therapy, either in the apartment building gym or the pool or at the recreation center downstairs or do yoga in the apartment. Then I'd eat a healthy breakfast, take a shower and shave, and rest until lunchtime, which usually included a couple of pieces of chocolate or an Indian dessert. After a nap and some tea or coffee, I'd go for an evening walk or meditate or listen to music or take a short trip somewhere with Sunita, whether shopping or to the Worli Sea Face, a famous promenade where we'd have coffee, sitting in the car. After dinner and some TV, I'd be in bed by 8:30 p.m. That was a day in the life of Sameer.

My dizziness levels continued to be high, but I was getting used to dealing with them. I still got struck with periods of depression when the "Why me?" thought would circle through my mind, but the periods were less intense than when I'd arrived, and certainly much less intense than they'd been the year before. I was making steady improvements in other areas, and with all the richness of the interactions with my friends and family and with meaningful activities, I was grateful each day to be alive.

Life Back Home

Even though I was with my loving mom, Sunita, and Dhananjay in the city where I grew up, I was missing my family and my life back home in Virginia. With April approaching, I knew Monica was grappling with an immense stack of paperwork, including taxes and Social Security claims, and I was grateful to her for handling all of it. I was able to help a little by filling out our son Jai's financial aid forms, and it felt good to be able to contribute.

Monica informed me that Arjun had been one of the two students selected at his school to get an award from the local chamber of commerce as recognition for his personal accomplishments. The award ceremony would be on the same day as his birthday. I felt so happy and sent him a gift card to the local mall as a reward. When the day came, I missed him terribly.

Monica, who knew I would be homesick, gently suggested that I extend my stay by six more weeks, and eventually, I agreed. I'd stay until the end of May instead of returning in early April. It did not make financial or tactical sense to go back in early April. Giving me six more weeks of therapy and care was the right decision, just as I had extended my stay in Nimba by a month in November. Sunita and

Dhananjay also agreed with the decision. Mak, my college friend, was going to visit India from New Jersey, and he graciously offered to help fly me back to DC.

Final Days and Homeward

The six-week extension of my stay meant I also got the chance to be with my mom on Mother's Day. I was happy to be with her and so were she and my sister. We took my mom to nearby Kebabs and Kurries, at the ITC Grand Central Hotel, for a Mother's Day brunch. But I was also sad to be away from the mom of my kids. I sent a gift certificate to the boys to give to their mom. I was happy with the progress I'd made during that second stay in India, and some of my strongest memories of that time are of significant milestones in my healing journey. My dear college friend Mohan picked me up one day and took me to visit our college, Podar, in the Matunga area of Mumbai. We had spent five years there in the mid-1980s, and we were nostalgic to go back. He was also kind enough to take me to one of my appointments with Dr. Khadilkar, and to Mak's parents' fiftieth anniversary party, which was the first time I had attended a big party since my surgery. Another milestone was when Sunita and Dhananjay took me to watch a movie in a theater. They had cautiously asked me if I would like to go, since they knew my dizziness and eye focus were challenges. It was highly liberating for me and gave me some confidence to continue to accept this new normal. We saw the Bollywood movie *Raid*, and I enjoyed it very much. I'm struck by how such an ordinary experience could have been so significant. Later, I went with Dhananjay to another Bollywood production, called *October*. I could not help but notice that both the movies had English titles. Like Americans, Indians are crazy about movies. Bollywood produces twice the movies Hollywood does annually, no matter what language the movie titles are in. It was another small step back to some normalcy. The brothers-in-law also got a chance to bond.

Another triumph was mounting curtain rods, using both my arms. It was a struggle because of the weakness on my left side. It was hard to raise my left hand above my head, and I was tempted to call someone to help me, but I wanted to see if I could do it myself. I wanted to be self-sufficient since I knew that in my life back in DC I would need to be more independent.

During my stay in India, I was able to drive a car for the first time after surgery—just two laps around Sunita's apartment building with Vikas next to me! This was huge for me. I love cars, just as my sons do, and I really loved and enjoyed driving before my stroke. It was another big step.

With my return flight approaching, I was happy to have gained enough strength to be able to spend a few hours with Sunita shopping for myself in the well-known Palladium Mall, where I also bought gifts for Monica and the boys. Sunita also took me to a local grocery store called Ashok Masala Stores. She knew that I was not a big foodie, so she sold me on going to the store by saying that even I would find their food products interesting and innovating.

My new mantra for the past year was "try everything," so I said, "Let's go." She was genuinely surprised I agreed to go. The place had innovative food mixes, ready-to-eat meals, different food products you don't get elsewhere—even this non-foodie was impressed. We also ordered medications to carry with me, which were substantially cheaper in India than back home.

Monica and Jai cautiously asked me if I should extend my stay beyond May as I was still experiencing dizziness. Just as I had asked Dr. Shyam at Nimba, I asked Dr. Khadilkar if staying another month or two made sense. He did not know when my dizziness would start subsiding, if at all. It could be two months, six months, a year or two, or never. He also counseled me with practical advice by asking me, "Where is your life?" He said, "If it's here, stay; if it's back in the States, go." I would have stayed in a heartbeat if doing so would have helped with my dizziness, but nobody knew if it would. I talked to Sunita, Dhananjay, and my mom about what to do, and they said they would support whatever I wanted. I made the decision to go back home as planned. It had been four months since I left Virginia, and I was homesick.

I had my final visit with Dr. Khadilkar, who was happy about my progress. I thanked him for all his help and asked him to look me up if he ever came to the US. Then it was also time for my final sessions with Nagesh, Harish, Dinesh, and Priyanka. These were bittersweet moments. I was sad that I would no longer be seeing these kind and compassionate people who had tirelessly worked to support my rehab for the previous four months, but I was also excited about going home, and I had significant milestones in my recovery to celebrate as well. I'd extended my swimming ability from one lap to eight laps, nonstop, and the biggest triumph of all was that steep slope in the driveway, which I'd vowed to conquer before I left. During my last session with Priyanka, I decided to tackle it. I started at the top, and with the help of my cane and my full concentration and effort, I was able to make it not only down to the bottom, but also to turn around and climb back to the top. It was tough, but the feeling upon reaching the top was worth every effort I'd put in over the last four months!

I also started to groom myself for the trip by getting a haircut and shave at home, courtesy of the local hairdresser who came to visit me. I realized that this kind of luxury would not be possible back home in Virginia, and that I would be going back to the "self-service" model. I began packing for my trip. It was a milestone to pack by myself.

One of the things which Sunita and I had talked about for four months was to visit the Siddhivinayak Temple across the street from her building. In my last days there, we finally went over and took Lord Ganesha's blessings, and then it was time for me to return home. My last day in Mumbai was also Sahil's birthday. He was visiting from Pune, and we had a celebration with him, with a small cake.

Finally, it was time for me to go to the airport. It was a bittersweet moment. I was excited to see my family in Virginia, but after four months, I would miss my family here in Mumbai. Dhananjay and Sunita had bought an apartment outside Mumbai near Pune, which had a nice golf course.

It hadn't been possible this trip for me to go there, but I told them I'd do it one fine day. With heavy hearts, we went to pick up Mak, my chaperone for the trip back. On the return flight, I took stock of my rehab over the previous four months and was happy with my progress. It was time to continue with the next phase of my recovery back home with my family.

• • •

"Take control of your destiny. Believe in yourself. Ignore those who try to discourage you. Avoid negative sources, people, places, things, and habits. Don't give up and don't give in."

—WANDA HOPE CARTER

Health Recovery Level

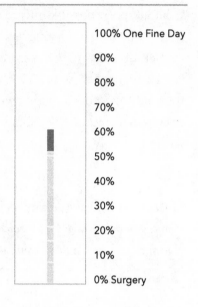

100% One Fine Day

90%

80%

70%

60%

50%

40%

30%

20%

10%

0% Surgery

SAMEERISM • Try everything with an open mind. My overall philosophy has been to try different remedies and therapies, whether in Western or Eastern medicine.

CHAPTER 7

It Is What It Is

*"To expect the unexpected, shows
a thoroughly modern intellect."*

OSCAR WILDE

I genuinely appreciated Mak escorting me back to Virginia where we arrived safe and sound. He left that same evening by Amtrak to go back to New Jersey. I am blessed and lucky to have had these kind folks to escort me for my trips. And as I did for Kedar, Dhananjay, and Anil, I came up with my "top ten" observations regarding Mak during our journey back. Doing those "top ten" lists made me feel like my old self.

As much as my rehab in Mumbai was good and needed, I knew I needed to be back in the States to be with my family and friends and to resume my life. Finding my new normal meant building upon my old life while progressing into a future that was different from what I'd planned. Every phase would have its setbacks and triumphs.

After this trip, I felt my recovery was like a baseball game going into extra innings. Even if it would take until the eleventh or twelfth inning, I was certain I would win in the end. The game was difficult and frustrating at times, but I felt thankful for the opportunity just to be able to play.

Back home with my family, I was determined to continue my healing, doing my best to keep my recovery on track and using both Western and Eastern systems of medicine and exercises and added new rehab exercises I had learned in Mumbai. I continued my remote meditation sessions with Sagar. I scheduled appointments to see my neurologist, Dr. Manem, my internist, Dr. Rachel, and my clinical psychologist, Dr. Susan. Still, there were always reminders that I couldn't resume my old life. I had to turn down an invitation to attend a fiftieth anniversary celebration for my former employer Datatel (now called Ellucian). I had really wanted to go, but I knew that I wouldn't be comfortable in the middle of a big crowd. Learning my limits was part of the acceptance process.

At this point, I could tally up my hits and misses. There were still many things my stroke prevented me from doing. I still couldn't drive a car a significant distance, wear my contact lenses, wear regular trousers, or drink my favorite single-malt Scotch. Working—even from home— wasn't possible. My progress over the past sixteen months had been undeniable; returning to the way things had been wasn't an option. Acceptance of my new normal—a state of being that kept changing and surprising me—was an ongoing challenge.

Then there was a major twist in my life, and my new

normal was changing once again. Monica and I decided to separate. I was certainly taken aback, and it took me some time to fully accept the fact, but eventually I did. I never thought in my wildest imagination this could ever happen to us. It was no doubt a tough decision to make, and it was very sad and unfortunate for both of us and the boys—we had known each other for more than half our lives. I believe we were good friends and had a good relationship. We had some normal husband-wife challenges before my stroke, but with my illness, we developed further cracks in our relationship. I thought we could work it out, but it was obvious to me that it was best to separate at this point, no matter how hard it was for all of us. I have no desire to share anything beyond this. All I want to say is you can't clap with one hand, and that no one but Monica and I are responsible for this painful decision. We were indeed blessed to have two wonderful kids whom we are both proud of. I am deeply grateful for all the help Monica has provided during my illness. I wish her well and all of us well and hope we all will heal. I urged her to continue writing. I had always thought her writing was good, and this situation didn't change any of that. For-tunately, Monica and I kept our separation amicable for the sake of our kids. However, the news of us separating did shock many of our friends and family.

The thought "Why me? Why us?" started to resurface, as it had in the first few months after my stroke. The dif-ference between now and then was that I was a little more accepting of reality. I was indeed sad, but not depressed. As painful and hard as this was, the phrase "it is what it is" continued to be my mantra, and now I added a new one: "Never say never." I remembered the good things we shared together over the years, thanked God for them, and prayed for our healing.

It seemed best that I find an apartment nearby and allow Monica and the kids to remain in our home. Jai agreed to drive me around to see different rental possibilities in the neighborhood. I was grateful for his help, though it was a hard experience for both of us. Jai's life was taking a positive turn at this point. He had started working as an intern for an analytics company in the same office building in Alexandria and on the same floor where my office at Grant Thornton was located. It was incredible. What are the chances of that? As we drove around, I passed along tips about places to eat and park near where he'd be working. I was immensely proud of my son for getting an internship after his freshman college year and wanted to help him in any way I could, even as he was helping me through a difficult time.

In spite of what was happening, I was determined to maintain my rehab program and stay involved in as many daily activities as possible. I felt great that I was able to help Monica a little with folding laundry and making tea for the two of us as she continued making us meals. It felt really nice to also do some paperwork, arrange for a contractor to do home repairs, watch my favorite series, *Homeland*—all ordinary things you could easily take for granted but miss if you were unable to do them. My friend Emanuele took me to the local swimming pool so I could practice the aqua therapy exercises I'd learned in Mumbai. With the help of

Jai and my friends Sal and Ron, I resumed my visits to Sam's barbershop for haircuts.

I was entering the fiftieth year of my life with a big milestone birthday slated for 2019. Monica and the boys bought me a nice cake. I was genuinely happy to celebrate with my family. Even as I enjoyed the day with them, I couldn't help but think that next year would be different.

There were other small but important achievements for me during this time. Strolling through a Best Buy store with Arjun and Jai, and seeing *Incredibles 2* with them on Father's Day was especially meaningful.

Moving day came. The apartment I had rented a few miles away was waiting for me. I had gone through the painful but necessary process of clearing out my closets, opening a new bank account, turning on the utilities, and ordering new furniture online. Packing for the move and the move itself were two of the most emotionally wrenching experiences of my life and my family's. I had lived in this home with them for sixteen years, and now it was time to leave. Jai and I agreed that it would be best for him not to help me move—it was too sad an occasion for both of us. Ron, Sal, and Kedar agreed to lend a hand. I was thankful to them for being there for me at such a difficult time.

Kedar stayed overnight to help me unpack and settle in before he drove back to New Jersey. He took me to a Target store to buy some needed items. It made me chuckle to see two childhood friends struggling to decide on what things to buy. (Kedar made an SOS call to Vrinda, who helped to guide our shopping.) Sal took me to Walmart for further needed purchases. Jai and Arjun came over to help me finish unpacking. It wasn't easy for them or for me. Accepting this new normal was something we shared together.

As I became used to my new apartment, I realized that this was the first time I had lived on my own; when I was single, I had always had roommates. I was glad to have found an apartment complex that made the transition a bit easier. There was a gym downstairs that was available to me twenty-four hours a day. Also critical was having a washer and dryer in my apartment. Sal installed an iron rod in the bathroom to make it easier to take a shower.

If I needed groceries, I could order through Instacart and have them delivered right to my kitchen. If I needed to go out, I could use Uber.

Overall, I was able to find ways to take care of my basic needs so I could concentrate on continuing my recovery.

As I was settling into my new normal, I ended my employment with Grant Thornton by taking a separation package. It was nice of them to keep my job as long as they had, and it was not fair to have them keep it open for more time, as my returning to work didn't look feasible in the foreseeable future. Although it was logical and the right thing to do, it was another milestone in my new normal, one I hadn't thought of or looked forward to reaching. Dave went out of his way to stay in touch, which meant a lot to me.

When you are sidelined from work and normal activities, it is easy to feel distant from friends and colleagues—worse, you might become an object of pity. Around this time, I started to notice a certain schadenfreude (a German word for taking pleasure in someone else's misfortune) in folks I didn't expect it from. It wasn't expressed directly. I picked up on it by reading between the lines in what they said and how they acted. At first, I took it personally. "How can they?" I thought. But over time, I realized that schadenfreude is just part of human nature, something you will have to face. I learned to accept it and moved on, as hard it was.

I still joked with my care providers about finding that magic pill. My body strength on my left side and my vision had significantly improved over time, but my dizziness was still severe. I felt as dizzy as I did right after my surgery. I joked with Ron and Sal, "I am intoxicated without alcohol." You couldn't tell I was experiencing dizziness from looking at my face, though. My stroke was on my cerebellum and affected my motor functions. My challenge was to accept and live with this dizziness and lack of balance until my brain healed. No one could say with certainty when that would be.

Sticking to a routine helped me cope with the challenges I faced. I looked forward to my weekly remote guided meditation sessions with Sagar. It had been nearly a year since I'd first worked with him at Nimba. Since then, we had grown close. Though he was not highly trained in psychology like Dr. Susan, I confided in him in a similar way. My guided meditation sessions became important to me. He offered more than therapeutic techniques—his whole being radiated calmness and peace. I would say to him, "You are like a guru to me." He'd say, "I'm not a guru—that's too strong a word. I'm more of a friend to you." Sagar calls me *Dada*, which, as noted earlier, means "elder brother" in my mother tongue, Marathi. Whatever you call it, I'm grateful for the relationship of trust and understanding we've built together.

As I looked around my new apartment, I saw the beginnings of the next chapter in my life. I counted my blessings even as I faced the hard work of continued recovery. When I had returned from Mumbai, I thought I knew what my new normal was going to be. It turned out to be something totally different. No matter. It is what it is. I was prepared for unexpected twists and turns, for more extra innings and hard-won victories. And I knew I would keep moving forward. I had to.

• • •

"It is through gratitude for the present moment that the spiritual dimension of life opens up."

—ECKHART TOLLE

Health Recovery Level

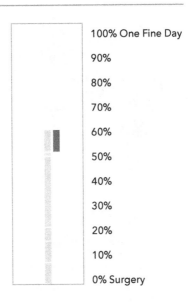

100% One Fine Day

90%

80%

70%

60%

50%

40%

30%

20%

10%

0% Surgery

SAMEERISM • No matter what adversity one faces, the first step is to accept it, as hard as it may be, and most importantly, find ways to move forward and face your new normal with gratitude.

CHAPTER 8

My New Normal

"Life is a balance of holding on and letting go."

RUMI

As I settled into my new normal at Avalon, the apartment community where I rented a one-bedroom apartment, I made sure to go to the gym downstairs for thirty to forty minutes on alternate days. "No fall," which the therapists used to say, was firmly entrenched in me. It was something I kept in mind during each workout. I had time to think and notice things about the world—and myself. One thing I clearly noticed was that my Indian accent was stronger than before. It had been there before my stroke, of course; but now, I could hear it more distinctly. The fact that I was not working in mainstream corporate America and had spent so much time in India may have had something to do with this. Now I sounded more like my favorite character Raj on the hit TV series *The Big Bang Theory*. (I love all the characters on that show, but Raj especially as I feel a connection with him, although I am not that geeky.) Interestingly enough, the actor Kunal Nayyar's book *Yes, My Accent Is Real*, is really witty and good. It reminds me that we go back to our roots when we are faced with adversity. I had always said, "You are what you are." Now I was living it. I guess, even though I've been in America for thirty years, you can't take the Indian out of me. This doesn't apply just to Indians. I think many folks, no matter whether they are locals or immigrants, will agree. It took this illness for me to realize more of my Indian-ness.

Being different in how you look, talk, or dress doesn't make you any less of an American, of course. You don't have to speak with an American accent or eat apple pie or a hamburger or do American things to prove your American-ness. Everyone has something about them that makes them stand out. The important thing is that everyone be judged as an individual who has value and something to contribute to their society. This applies no matter who you are, and not just in India or the US but anywhere in the world. Through all my travels, no matter where I was, I saw the goodness in almost everyone I met. It's a lesson that has come through even more clearly as I've worked on my recovery.

I used to discuss with my father why our last name, in spite of consisting of just five letters, was so difficult for people to pronounce, not just in the US but also in our native India and in Germany, where he was posted for five years by his bank. I'll bet my kids feel the same way. The pronunciation I've heard in the States over the last thirty years sounded either like *bidet* or *behide*. I was okay with the many different pronunciations folks would use. But in the last few years, I finally started telling people what the real pronunciation was. Since there is no sound in the English language for *bh*, "bee-day" is the closest. I think many people from different ethnicities and backgrounds—not just folks from different nationalities, but also from different regions of our nation—have similar challenges, and not just in their names, but also with other things about them that might set them apart. That's bound to happen.

My frequent use of Uber illustrated this for me. I used Uber extensively to go to different appointments and therapies, among other places. One of the best things about Uber, besides its convenience, is the chance it gives you to talk to the many drivers who are from different parts of the world, including different regions of the States. Little things have reminded me of our common humanity. A few months after I moved into Avalon, when an Uber driver was dropping me off, he noticed that my jeans had come loose. He saw that I needed some assistance to pull them back up and offered his help without my asking. I don't think he cared what my color or religion was. It was a simple act of kindness—not a big deal but still very meaningful. Thinking of others isn't a special quality of any single culture. I've encountered it all over the world for the most part.

I've found this in the community at Avalon. Right away, I was impressed by the staff's diversity as well as their kindness. Black and white, locals and foreign-born, different religions and nationalities, from Latin America, the

Caribbean, and Africa, it doesn't matter. From what I've seen, everyone works well together, despite coming from different cultures and speaking different languages. This to me is the real America, the one I am proud to be a part of.

Djafar, the office manager, was from Senegal. He carried boxes up to my apartment on the day I moved in. It wasn't his responsibility, but he was happy to help. After my furniture was delivered and assembled, he also helped me dispose of the boxes. Djafar was about thirty-five or forty, with two sons. We bonded well. It was sad to see him go after he took a job elsewhere.

I developed a good rapport with Sandy, Avalon's concierge. She's from Trinidad, a woman of Indian origin. (Many folks in the Caribbean have Indian origins.) I would see her nearly every day, and we grew to be friends. She took an interest in my health and always encouraged me to use the gym. She's the kind of person who goes beyond her job description to help people. There was the time I forgot my phone in an Uber driver's car. When she heard what happened, she volunteered to help me get it back. I can count on Sandy to open the door for me when my ride arrives. She doesn't have to do that, but she does anyway. I know a lot of people at Avalon appreciate her kindness.

I also started making some new friends. One of them is Thierry Sagnier, a Frenchman and an established author who lives on my floor. He encouraged me regarding my health progression. Thierry and I would grab coffee or lunch, and he would give me valuable advice on writing *One Fine Day*, as he himself had written seven books.

I was fortunate to be able to include good people like Djafar, Sandy, and Thierry in my new normal. Not just the Avalon office staff was nice, but so were many folks in maintenance, like Blanca and Alba from El Salvador, and outside providers like the mailman, Mr. Gene, and the Amazon delivery person. Mr. Gene sorted out a mail-forwarding problem for me and was always pleasant to speak with. He has since retired from the US Postal Service. I wish him well.

One day, I saw the Amazon delivery person in the lobby doing his rounds. He was wearing a smashing Amazon T-shirt. I said, "I like your T-shirt. It looks great."

He said, "Thanks. Would you like one? If so, tell me your size."

I told him, but never thought in a million years he would get me one. The next day, the shirt was waiting for me with Sandy. I was blown away by his act of generosity. As a loyal Amazon customer, I loved this simple act by an empowered employee. I thought again, "This is our real America."

The Avalon staff could only help me so much. I had to depend upon myself for most of my day. There were things I'd learned to do to both strengthen my body and sustain my spirit. I would start my mornings by lighting a candle and saying a simple prayer for God's blessing in front of the Hindu god idols I keep in my kitchen. While I am not intensely religious, I've been doing this for many years. It makes me feel calmer and brings me a sense of peace. When I was in Mumbai, one of my mother's friends, Mrs. Barwe, gave me a Lord Ganesh Aarti music box. It is an electric music device that plays prayers to the Lord Ganesh. It became part of my morning ritual to plug in the box and say my prayers and then make coffee while the music ran in the background. It gave me the extra strength and courage I needed to face the day ahead.

The difficult moments continued but so did the small triumphs. I was cooking on my own a little more, making things like smoothies, sandwiches, salads, and *kande pohe*, a classic dish from my region of India. I was able to operate the dishwasher and do laundry on my own. I continued doing paperwork—bank statements, Grant Thornton benefits, insurance, legal papers, Social Security claims, and the like. I called, texted, emailed, and had lunch, dinner, or coffee with friends and acquaintances whenever I could. Friends continued to help me go to some therapy sessions, the barber, and doctor appointments, or make CVS Pharmacy runs and take other trips around the area. I could manage most of the tasks in the apartment quite well, but I found taking a bath in the bathtub definitely challenging, as I had had a shower stall in the house. But I managed it. The rod Sal installed was a lifesaver.

Not all my challenges involved everyday tasks. Getting out and meeting new people wasn't easy for me. Avalon hosted a pancake breakfast for residents in the lobby. At first, I thought my dizziness would keep me from going. But I made a point to go and enjoyed talking with some of the people there. I was glad I was able to attend. I could see that Avalon's residents were as diverse as the staff. The apartment complex was a microcosm of our America.

Keeping my recovery moving forward was an ongoing task. Living on my own meant taking more direct control of my medical regimen. Because going to Dr. Susan was helpful, I started scheduling visits with her on my own for the first time. I also resumed my visits with Dr. Manem, who monitored my progress. I became friendly with her receptionist, Afroze. She was from Multan, Pakistan. I knew a little bit about Multan since Monica's family had been from there before the partition of the subcontinent in 1947. We conversed in Hindi and Urdu, both pretty much the same language although they use different scripts. As an Indian and a Pakistani, we were not supposed to get along. But we did. We were not unique in this. Most Indians and Pakistanis will feel the same, especially here in the States. Although separated by religion, we are the same people culturally. I also found a cleaning service owned by Luly from Bolivia. Like the apartment staff and residents, her crew was also diverse with ladies from different countries. Hay House, my favorite publisher, was offering four free master classes online about how to be an author, so I made a point to attend those. After taking those classes, the inspiration for *One Fine Day* solidified further.

Still trying to control my dizziness, I went to see my neurosurgeon, Dr. Vyas, one last time. He referred me to Dr. Monafred, an ENT specialist in Reston, Virginia, who recommended I begin aggressive vestibular therapy as well as taking vitamins to see if they would help. The vestibular system contains part of the inner ear and the brain, and provides balance and eye movements. I began the vestibular sessions at Select Physical Therapy in Annandale, Virginia. It was there that I met the queen.

Her Royal Highness the Queen, the name I used to tease her, was Anne Marie. She took charge of my case as soon as I started booking appointments at Select Physical. There was a sign in her office that said, "The Queen Will See You Now," given to her by one of her patients. It made me chuckle, and I took to calling her the Queen of Therapy. There was no doubt she was in command of the facility, but that didn't make her any less of a caring person. I found her easy to talk to. She was from Boston, and had a good Boston accent, so naturally the subject of the New England Patriots kept coming up. Our rapport made the therapy sessions go easier. Every queen should be as nice as Anne Marie! The other staff at Select Physical were also truly kind and nice—Cynthia, Elizabeth, and Allison.

For the first few days after I moved, I didn't have a TV and cable service, which was a new experience. It was odd not having a TV, but I did not miss it much. In fact, it was quite relaxing—especially not watching the news. Eventually, I did get one, but decided not to get cable service. Instead, I signed up for Internet TV (YouTube TV) for the first time. I wanted to be cable-free for a while. I started to watch less news, and it was a huge change for me.

Relaxation was a big part of my healing. After my surgery, my doctors advised me that to rest my brain, it was essential to take regular naps in the afternoon. I took time out to enjoy watching my favorite movies and TV shows on Amazon Prime and Netflix at whatever time I could, since I could do so only on a limited basis due to my health condition. *Jack Ryan*, *The Widow*, and *The Man in the High Castle* were some of my favorites. I also enjoyed Bollywood content (especially *Sacred Games*, one of Netflix India's popular series) and listening to books downloaded from Audible. Sports continued to be a passion for me. The beginning of football season meant cheering on the Washington Redskins again and exchanging texts about the game and the season with Jai. I remained a baseball and cricket fan as well. I also continued with my passion for helping people network and find job opportunities.

Family and friends still meant the world to me. Living on my own made me deeply grateful for the times I could spend with them. It was important to be with my kids, especially on special occasions. I celebrated Jai's birthday by taking him and Arjun out for bowling and pizza at our regular bowling alley. After Monica's and my separation, holidays and special days could be tough—that was one of the hardest things about my new normal. The date of what would have been our milestone anniversary came a few days after I moved to Avalon. I especially missed my family on holidays like Thanksgiving, Labor Day, Christmas, the Indian festival of Diwali, and days such as Halloween and the first day of school. Fortunately, friends stepped in and made me feel welcome. Being invited to share Thanksgiving dinner with Ron and Britt made the day special. Visits from Mak, Meghana, and Vrinda from New Jersey and Anil and Aparna from Boston helped brighten the late fall and winter of 2018. I had used Facebook and LinkedIn before my stroke, but not much. Because many folks did not know what had happened to me, after a hiatus of two and a half years, I started using those apps a little to keep friends and family in the loop about what was going on in my life. I also started sharing "lessons learned" from my journey. I called them Sameerisms and posted them once a week. I received good feedback and found they were helping some people, which was my goal.

My dizziness kept me from attending a Christmas brunch at my friend Susan's home. I also was not able to attend Christmas Eve church services with Kapil and his wife, Sharon. On Anne Marie's recommendation, I started vision therapy for my nystagmus with Dr. Cantwell in Annandale. Both Dr. Cantwell and my therapist, Richard, were kind and worked diligently on my therapy. New Year's Eve found me staying home and watching the ball drop on TV. I wondered what 2019 would bring and how much progress I would make in my recovery. I had come a long way since my stroke. Whatever happened, I was going to approach life with a spirit of gratitude. I wanted to show my appreciation for those who had helped me and stood by me. On January 31 —the second anniversary of my brain surgery—I sent out thank-you emails to many people who had helped me over the past two years.

It was especially important to me to give back to Fairfax Inova Hospital in some way. I owed my life to them. I had donated some money, but I wanted to do more. The staff suggested that I join the Patient Family Advisory Council (PFAC), a volunteer group of ex-patients that offers suggestions about how Inova can improve its services. I started attending meetings (generally two-hour sessions held monthly) at the hospital. One of the first things I worked on was helping with designing a brochure to hand out to patients and caregivers. I knew some design experts who worked on projects like this and asked them to offer some ideas. It felt good to draw upon my experience and contacts. I wanted to be useful in whatever ways I could.

Most of the people who served on the council had stayed at Inova for five to seven days. I was the only one who had been in the ICU for a month and another month at Inova Mount Vernon. I had joked about becoming a legend at Nimba for being there for so long—it was the same at Inova. However, I don't think I received any special attention at the meetings because of that. All feedback was looked upon as equal feedback. Overall, it's been very satisfying to be part of the PFAC. If my health permitted, I would do even more. PFAC member Maggie Broadwater made this statement: "We were fortunate to have Four Fs—faith, family, friends, and Fairfax—on our side." I couldn't agree more.

My time with friends continued to be a blessing in my life. I was glad to be able to plan a milestone birthday celebration for my friend Ron at a restaurant close by along with some of our close friends. I was looking forward to attending a surprise fiftieth birthday party for Kedar in New Jersey. When dizziness prevented me from taking Amtrak, I told Vrinda I could not go. She offered to drive four hours to pick me up and take me to their home, all without Kedar knowing what was up. While packing my stuff, I felt like a kid in a dorm, going home for a break. Kedar was completely surprised that I was there to help him celebrate. I was so happy to share this milestone birthday with my old and dear friend. He drove me back to Virginia the following weekend.

Being a part of my sons' lives as they grew up was a priority. Arjun and I went to the Washington Auto Show with Ron and Sal. I am forever indebted to them for taking us and wheeling me around. Arjun enjoyed checking out the various cars and rides at this annual event. (We had attended the show together in previous years, but I was not able to go in 2018.) It had become our annual ritual. Arjun's birthday was the same month, and I ordered a cake and his favorite foods from Olive Garden, and celebrated with him and Jai at my apartment. I was able to see Arjun perform as emcee at his school's variety show via Twitter. Arjun was excelling at his studies, and I gave him a gift certificate as a reward. Jai was also excelling academically at his university and got on the dean's list. My happiness went through the roof. I was proud of the boys doing so well during these very tough times. I thought, "Monica and I must have done something right to deserve sons like these."

My milestone fiftieth birthday was coming up. I wanted to celebrate with a party that would express my thanks to twenty or so key friends for their extraordinary help over the past two difficult years. Britt and Ron pitched in to help organize the event. Anil came down from Boston and also lent a hand. The party was held in the Avalon rec room. Kedar, Vrinda, Mak, and Meghana drove down to take part in the fun. Really, I was just grateful to be alive to reach my half-century mark. I had asked them to share photos of themselves with me, and I created a slideshow complete with background music of my favorite Michael Jackson songs, which I played during the celebration. Instead of birthday gifts, I requested donations be made to Inova Hospital System for me. (Inova is a nonprofit organization.)

The one thing my friends couldn't give me for my birthday was a magic pill to cure me completely. My search for that magic pill continued. It was up to me to manage my recovery and consider different ways to heal. Anne Marie suggested I try physical therapy at Select Physical's Mc-Lean, Virginia facility, where they had a new trainer who had worked with rehabbing stroke patients. This is where I met Alex. I did a few physical therapy sessions with him. Even though he was half my age, we bonded pretty well. He was truly kind and good at his craft. My friend Beth asked her neurosurgeon friend Dr. Rocco Armando at MedStar Hospital in DC if he had any recommendations for my dizziness issues. He thought I should enter the rehab program at MedStar Hospital. Dr. Guillermety, a physiatrist (a physician trained in physical medicine and rehabilitation) at MedStar DC, thought I should start vestibular therapy again and recommended that the MedStar Stroke Center look at my reports. I asked her about taking CBD (cannabidiol) oils, and she recommended I try them. I began taking a few drops of CBD oil every day. I told my caregivers, "If it does not kill me, I would like to try it." As summer approached, I wanted my recovery level to continue to improve. For all the progress I'd made, though, the danger of slipping backward remained real.

I wanted to find ways of turning the negatives in my life into a positive. Telling my story felt like a way of doing that—most importantly, it might offer strength and encouragement to others facing any life change or adversity. But I was not sure how I would write due to my health condition. I could not type with two hands and could not focus on my laptop more than ten or fifteen minutes at a stretch. I found a way to do it by hiring a professional ghostwriter to write it for me. I would be the author of my stories and experiences, and the ghostwriter would write it for me. I was reliving the ups and downs of my story even as I prepared a book proposal and outline. I could see that becoming an author was as much of a personal journey as the process of healing.

On one beautiful day, I walked from my bank near the Dunn Loring Metro Station back to my apartment. I used the new cane I had ordered online at Anne Marie's recommendation. It was only a half-mile walk, but it was a huge milestone for me. Another big milestone was when I walked down four flights of stairs with the cane because of a false fire alarm at my apartment complex. (There were also many other false fire alarms later on, which tested my strength and ability.) I savored these small triumphs and wished I could keep going forward at an unbroken pace.

But I knew my new normal had to be lived one day and one step at a time.

The cane was a big part of my new normal. I joked with someone, "As long as I have my girlfriend with me I am good," referring to the cane. The look on the person's face was priceless. They were probably thinking, "Here is a married man, with a severe disability, openly talking about having a girlfriend." When I told the person who the girlfriend was, we both burst out laughing. Frankly, the cane to me was like a girlfriend: always with me. If it could talk, I'd bet it would nag me for sure.

• • •

"The secret of life isn't what happens to you, but what you do with what happens to you."

—NORMAN VINCENT PEALE

Health Recovery Level

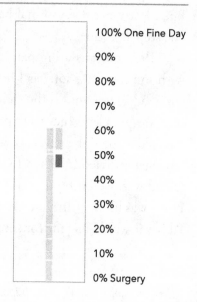

100% One Fine Day

90%

80%

70%

60%

50%

40%

30%

20%

10%

0% Surgery

SAMEERISM • Learn to balance independence in your recovery with accepting help from others.

CHAPTER 9

Change Is the Only Normal

"We may all have come on different ships,
but we are in the same boat now."

DR. MARTIN LUTHER KING, JR.

My new normal changed once again when my dizziness, balance, and headaches increased noticeably. The spike persisted, so five days later, I called the paramedics and had them take me to the ER at Fairfax Inova Hospital. During the five-minute ride, my thoughts went back to January 31, 2017, when we made a similar call to the paramedics, and I made the same trip over the same road to the same ER. Being back in the ambulance and going to the same ER was a strange sort of déjà vu, but this time I did not pass out. I couldn't help but worry that I was slipping backward in my recovery. It had been slow and arduous so far, but what if there was something dramatically new that was wrong with me?

I was at the ER for about three or four hours. The CAT scan room looked familiar, even though I had been passed out the first time I'd been there and then was in a medically induced coma after my two brain surgeries. Later, I found they had taken me to the CAT scan room multiple times before and after the surgeries.

Waiting for the results kept me on edge. Finally, the doctor on staff told me that the test was clear with no new bleeding evident, but there was just no explanation for the spike in dizziness and headaches. I definitely felt relieved, but was still very concerned and frustrated. My mantra remained "it is what it is," as hard it was. But that didn't keep me from worrying that something had changed—and not for the better.

Frustrated, I tried to distract myself by watching TV for whatever time I could manage: the FIFA Women's World Cup in France (so proud of the US team who won it all), the Cricket World Cup in England, Netflix and Amazon shows (season two of *Jack Ryan* being my favorite). August brought another huge milestone for me: I started writing *One Fine Day* with Barry Alfonso, my ghostwriter with kn literary arts, a top writing professional, and a gentle and kind person.

Within a week of my ER visit, I saw Dr. Richard Benson, a neurologist at the MedStar Stroke Center referred by Dr. Guillermety. The CBD oil she had recommended didn't seem to help very much, but I kept taking it, hoping that it might work one fine day. As she had suggested, I started vestibular therapy again. But it increased my dizziness, so I stopped.

Dizziness and headaches sidelined me from visits to the gym for many days. Tired of not working out, I started up again, putting in ten minutes of elliptical exercise and twenty minutes on the stationary bike—my standard workout regime. It was exceedingly difficult with my dizziness and headaches, but I managed to do it for several weeks. I also resumed therapy with Alex.

I was so desperate for the dizziness to go away, I tried drinking a regular beer for relief—maybe having some alcohol would have a reverse effect. Before my stroke, I would have a beer or a glass of wine (okay, maybe three or four) a couple of days a week. After my stroke, my doctors had discouraged me from consuming any alcohol, as the first thing it does is affect the brain. (I guess that's why people drink in the first place.) But it had been a strict no. Having a regular beer—a Stella Artois, to be exact—was a milestone. It didn't seem to help or hurt, but I did enjoy it.

Around this time, my Social Security disability claim was approved, and half of the monthly benefits go directly to Arjun, which is such a huge help for us. What a relief it was! Over all the years I was working, like many people, I used to grumble about all the payroll deductions (FICA, Social Security, and Medicare) from my paycheck. I felt really good when I realized these benefit payments are not a handout by the government, but are based on what I'd paid in to the Social Security system for more than twenty years. Approval from the Social Security Administration also meant I was eligible for Medicare, which had substantial lower premiums than the very expensive COBRA premiums I was paying—although the private plan was great. Both Social Security and Medicare can be improved; they are not perfect. I am not advocating for or against them, just honestly acknowledging the fact that they are saving my ass.

My new normal continued to change. I experienced another bout of increased dizziness, balance issues, and headaches. This time, the pain was concentrated on the incision point of my surgery at the lower back side of my head. I stopped going to the gym. This new spike continued for seven days before I went back to the ER for another exam. Our friend Lydia was kind enough to drive me there. Once again, my CAT scan was clear.

The two ER visits over the summer made me think, "What if something happens to me?" I created a will and a living will (medical directive) using the LegalZoom website. I assigned primary and secondary executors and told them where the wills were. I also created a spreadsheet called "Post SBB" (my initials) on my laptop with information on the various accounts I had and what I wanted done with them if I died. I told the appropriate people how to access my laptop and the spreadsheet. This is something my father had done before he passed away, and it was useful to my mom to understand and navigate their financial information after his passing.

Still seeking relief, I made an appointment to see Dr. Mostofi, a neurologist in Vienna, Virginia. I was hoping to receive biofeedback treatment from him, but instead he suggested nerve block shots to my temples. He couldn't guarantee they would ease my headaches, but I thought they were worth a try. Dr. Mostofi and his receptionist, Maryam, were originally from Iran. I knew a little about Iran as my ex-boss in Boston, Javad, was from there, so we talked a little about their beautiful country. Like Javad, both Dr. Mostofi and Maryam were intelligent and kind. Having two shots administered to my skull was probably the most dramatic treatment I'd tried to date, but once again, I was disappointed with the results. I didn't return for further shots.

As before, friends continued to help to sustain me through difficult times. Susan got my medicines from the pharmacy when I could not go due to my dizziness. She is an excellent cook and brought me some delicious food as well. Sal and Ron continued to give me moral support by hanging out with me whenever possible, and taking me to Sam, the barber, for my haircuts and running other errands. Kedar and Vrinda came down to drop their daughter off at a local college and stopped by for a surprise visit. They were worried about how I was doing and couldn't understand why the doctors couldn't figure out what was going on. I wished I could give them answers; I wished I had the answers myself. It was deeply frustrating, but I was determined to channel my frustration into something productive. I got a visit from the pig, Anil, a buddy from Iowa days. We used to refer to ourselves as PIGS (poor Indian graduate students), a term common with Indian international students in the States. His visit was great as we reminisced about our days in Des Moines. Fortunately, I could use my laptop to stay in touch with friends and let them know I had a positive attitude.

Although my new normal continued to bring me setbacks, there were also small triumphs. After not going to the gym for almost a month, I started working out again. Coincidentally (or not), I began to experience pain in my right shoulder along with another spike in dizziness and headaches. I had to give up my gym sessions again, but the pain didn't stop me from continuing to work on my book project and managing everyday tasks around the apartment. I took special pride in using the slow cooker (Instant Pot) that Kedar and Vrinda had given me back in June. It had been a real game-changer for me. I was able to make pasta, salmon, yogurt, rice, and other dishes that would've been difficult for me to manage otherwise. Jai and Arjun were stunned when I made them macaroni and cheese as a special treat one day. The reaction on their faces said, "Daddy can cook!" They had hardly ever seen me cook before.

Watching the Washington Nationals on TV as they made their way to the World Series that fall was a highpoint for me. I shared my excitement with Jai, who is as big a sports fan as I am. I told him, "You really should go to one of the World Series games. What are the chances this will happen again? You'll remember it for the rest of your life." He was not sure about going because tickets were quite expensive. It felt like a true father-son moment when I told him to just do it. If I had been up to it, I would've loved to have gone with him. I knew Jai would have loved that also. He made me feel a part of it all as he texted me and sent photos from the game. He had a great time and was glad he had gone. One fine day, we will go to a game.

I had a memorable meeting with Dr. Steve Narang, the new CEO of Inova Fairfax. I had first met him at the hospital's monthly advisory council meeting. During our private talk, I told him the story of my stroke and what had happened since. He said, "I can't believe you are sitting here in front of me. You went through such a massive surgery." Then he asked, "Did you know you were that strong? You have an incredible spirit and a unique ability to connect with others." I told him that my mother and grandmother were strong, so I guess I knew I could get through all this. I also added that three generations of Bhides had been patients at Inova: my father, myself, and Arjun, who was born at the hospital. Monica had been treated there as well. I joked that if Inova awarded frequent user points, I would have gotten them big time.

I had another small scare, but thankfully, it had nothing to do with my condition. My laptop got fried. I had lots of *One Fine Day* notes and data on there. Luckily, a local service provider, Total Tech Geeks, salvaged my data. I am eternally grateful to them.

Strength is something you don't fully know you have until you need it. But I've also seen how important empathy and compassion are. I've always valued these qualities, but they've become especially meaningful since my stroke. I think people who know me have noticed a change in me. That transformation was brought home by an old movie I saw. One of my mother's friends, Mrs. Thakur, who had known me since my childhood recommended I watch *Regarding Henry*, a 1991 film starring Harrison Ford. She thought I would relate to the story of its title character—and I certainly did.

Henry Turner is a successful and ruthless lawyer in New York City. He gets shot while buying a pack of cigarettes at a local convenience store. He survives the bullet wound to his head but loses all memory of his life, his family—everything. Before the shooting, he was kind of rude and aggressive, consumed with winning at all cost. As he goes through physical therapy, he transforms into a different and better human being. Harrison Ford portrayed Henry's character brilliantly.

Before my stroke, I was never as extreme as Henry, but I definitely saw some part of myself in the story.

One scene in the film especially appealed to me. Henry is upset when he overhears a group of people laughing at his inability to work due to his condition. He talks about how he feels to Bradley, the therapist who had worked with him on his recovery. Bradley says, "Don't listen to nobody trying to tell you who you are. It might take a while, but you'll figure yourself out." I heard strength and determination in those words. Finding a renewed purpose in life and not letting others define who you are sounded like the new normal I was living every day.

Another spike in dizziness and headaches struck me, which brought about another round of visits to doctors for tests and treatment. My right shoulder continued to bother me, so I went to Dr. Anthony Avery at OrthoVirginia for a cortisone shot. I told Jai I felt like Max Scherzer, the ace pitcher for the Washington Nationals. He had a similar shot before the start of game seven of the World Series. Unlike the shot had done for Max, it didn't ease my pain, so Dr. Avery ordered an MRI of my shoulder.

There were positive and enjoyable things that happened that month as well. Kedar picked me up the day before Thanksgiving to spend the holiday with his family in New Jersey, as well as to celebrate Vrinda's fiftieth birthday. (I was extremely proud of dear Vrinda for running the TCS New York City Marathon as a gift to herself to celebrate her milestone birthday.) We shared a wonderful birthday dinner at their home with their friends, and I took photos with my SLR camera for the first time since my stroke. We had a tasty Thanksgiving meal at their friend's home. I was tired but happy when Kedar's nephew Abhishek dropped me back home in Virginia.

Since the dizziness spike kept me from going to therapy or the gym, I kept myself occupied doing paperwork, watching Netflix, writing *One Fine Day* with Barry, and doing other activities in whatever limited time I could concentrate on them. Thierry, being an esteemed writer, was kind enough to agree to edit the chapters of the book as we wrote them. I hired him without any hesitation.

Even though the brain MRI Dr. Manem had ordered was clear, the shoulder MRI revealed a massive rotator cuff tear. Dr. Avery thought the tear was probably due to overuse over the last three years. Not to mention, I had also used the shoulder a lot when I played competitive badminton and cricket while growing up, and playing tennis and racquetball here in the States. Also, I had turned fifty. All of this may have contributed to the tear. Whatever the reasons, I had to take care of it, as it was my good side. Since the tear was quite big, Dr. Avery recommended surgery as the only option. My new normal was changing yet again. There was just no way I could have the surgery while living alone in my apartment in Virginia as my good arm would be in a sling for four to six weeks. I decided that Mumbai would be the best place to have the procedure done. My mom and sister would be there to help me, and the local home care folks and therapists were much more affordable. I had already made plans to visit India for an Offshore 3.0 visit. Now I extended it.

My mom gently suggested that I stay with her until the sling came off as it was going to be convenient for her, since her processes and systems in her apartment were in place. I agreed with her suggestion instantly, and she was shocked that I did so without any resistance. We decided I'd move to Sunita's after my sling came off. As I had two years before, I contacted my friend Dr. Antya Joshi of Sportsmed and sent him my MRI report. This time around, my case was more relevant for Sportsmed, and he agreed that, if his upper limb specialist confirmed the diagnosis, they would do the surgery at Sportsmed itself.

Dizziness hit me hard, but I was determined not to miss going to a Christmas Eve service with Kapil and Sharon for a second year in a row. I was glad I went. It was a beautiful service. On New Year's Eve, I watched Anderson Cooper and Andy Cohen on TV for the ball drop in Times Square and went to sleep at midnight. Goodnight, 2019.

On New Year's Day, I sent best wishes to friends and prayed that my levels of dizziness and headaches would come down in 2020. Getting ready to leave for Mumbai was now my main task. I was glad to make plans to fly out after the Super Bowl, which I did not want to miss. When my sister asked me, "Why not come earlier?" I told her, "I am busy." She started to ponder what I was so busy with if I was not working. It was indeed a good football game and, the half-time show with Shakira and Jennifer Lopez was definitely kick-ass. Ron and Britt had invited me over to join them for a Super Bowl party they were hosting. I decided not to go, as there would be many people I knew, and I would have to talk a lot, which would have given me more headaches and dizziness. So I watched the Super Bowl at home.

Before I left, I saw Dr. Susan and Dr. Manem and visited Dr. Carrie Dougherty at the MedStar Headache Center. Dr. Dougherty gave me some meds for my headache, but they didn't do the trick. She suggested Botox treatments for my headache after I returned.

I had enjoyable get-togethers for brunch or coffee with Chandu and Lydia, Vinu, and Thierry. Sal and Ron also took Arjun and me to the Washington Auto Show, as they had the year before.

As the date of my departure grew closer, I challenged myself to eat only what I had in the fridge and the pantry. It is amazing how much stuff we all have. It felt good to not waste food and to save money. I intend to do this once every couple of months as a regular practice.

A few days before my flight, I suffered yet another spike in dizziness and headaches, and the incision point of my surgery started to hurt more. Not wanting to take any chances, I visited the ER. This time, I didn't want to call the paramedics or trouble anyone else, so I managed to take an Uber. At the ER, I was given a medicine cocktail through an

IV as well as a CAT scan. I recognized the kind gentleman who took me for the CAT scan. Anthony from Ashanti, Ghana. I also recognized the medicine cocktail they gave me. It was kind of scary that I knew the folks and the meds in the ER, but I was glad that I could remember this loving man. I guess my brain cells were firing well. Even though ER visits are tough, it was good to see Anthony again. Luckily, the CAT scan was clear yet again—no existing bleed, no new bleed. Although the ER doctor was glad the CAT scan was clear, like Dr. Manem before him, he could not explain why the spike happened. I started to treat this as my new normal. "It is what it is," I kept saying to myself as Chandu picked me up to go home.

As I approached the three-year anniversary of my stroke, I definitely felt anxious. I also had some difficult conversations with my close friends about my lack of sex drive since my stroke. It was tough to discuss this very personal thing, as I never had discussed anything like this before with anyone, but I found talking to them relatively comfortable. In not making light of my very personal situation, as was my usual fashion, I tried to be humorous by saying, "I will be back one fine day."

Two days before my travels, my headache, dizziness, and balance issues spiked yet again. I started to worry whether I could even undertake the long journey. Since I was going to be gone for four months, I renewed my Avalon lease, which reminded me very much of my continuing new normal. Thierry stopped by to see me off. On the day of my departure, I decided to just go. There was no point in sitting at home. My issues would not go away. I was also glad to make mango *kulfi* (Indian gelato) for Lydia and Chandu, in spite of my dizziness and headache.

I gathered some strength and packed my two bags and went to the airport with my friend Kapil. I was excited to see my mother and sister in Mumbai, but also anxious about the long journey—my first on my own since the stroke—and the coronavirus, which had started to spread in the States, and the shoulder surgery waiting for me. I was going to have my strength and spirit tested yet again.

• • •

"My humanity is bound up in yours, for we can only be human together."

—DESMOND TUTU

Health Recovery Level

The first time in three years I felt that recovery was stalling.

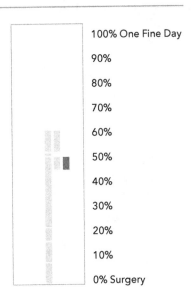

100% One Fine Day

90%

80%

70%

60%

50%

40%

30%

20%

10%

0% Surgery

SAMEERISM • If you see some "fatigue" in caregivers and friends related to their involvement or intensity in your care or interaction, don't take it personally. It is totally understandable as no one, including the person closest to you, can be there 100 percent of the time. Just understand that it does not mean their love has diminished, or that they care less for you. They are just human like you are. A lot of the time, people don't even realize it.

CHAPTER 10

The New Normal Shouldn't Be Taken for Granted

"Life is a series of natural and spontaneous changes, don't resist them; that only creates sorrow. Let reality be reality. Let things flow naturally forward in whatever way they like."

LAO TSU

Another chapter in my new normal began as I boarded the United Airlines flight at Washington Dulles. Even though it was not an Offshore 3.0 visit for rehab, it was still a medical visit, but for a different reason. Other than wheelchair assistance from the airline, I made it to the plane myself. My anxiety level was high, as this would be my first trip alone since my stroke. Though I knew one of my kind friends would have come with me in a heartbeat had I asked them, I felt it was time to travel on my own and not bother anyone else. It was a bit risky. Still, the sooner I accepted how things had to be, the better. But as I had done for the last three years, I was not going to take any risks. If I had even a remote doubt that I could not do it, I would have asked one of them to come. I promised them this once they found out I was going solo.

I had a pleasant and relaxing eight-hour flight from DC to London, enjoyed a delicious British shepherd's pie during the three-hour layover, then transferred to Air India for the second leg of the journey to Mumbai. My college friend Swati, an Air India senior air hostess, put in a good word for me with the crew, so I received extra special care. Particularly thoughtful were crew members Jyoti and Naresh, whom, for some reason, I kept calling Deepak during the flight. I only learned his correct name as we were about to land.

I managed to grab some sleep, ate the tasty meals they served on board, and luckily didn't suffer an increase in my dizziness or headache during the nine-hour flight. It was good to know I could make a long trip like this comfortably.

Sunita and Dhananjay were there to greet me outside the airport lounge when I arrived. We were all in a happy mood as we left the parking lot. I joked with their driver, Vikas, about his weight, just like I had two years earlier. We headed to my mom's apartment in midtown Mumbai. Mom was in tears when she saw me—it was the first time we'd been together in two years and the very first time since my divorce. We had a lot of catching up to do.

It took a few days for me to get over my jet lag and get used to living at my mom's place once again. Although it was the same apartment where I'd grown up and was well equipped with the comforts of home, it was still an adjustment to be back. I had no problem adjusting to mom's delicious home-cooked meals, though! As she helped me get around the apartment, I could not help but think about how she had taken such great care of my dad while he recovered from his heart ailment, and of my grandmother when her health had started to fail. It should have been my turn to help Mom, but now in her old age, she had to help me. It made me feel sad, but I guess this is how life goes. Mom seemed to take it all in stride. Now I know where my strength comes from.

I made myself useful by teaching her how to use email, her iPad, SMS, a karaoke app, and other everyday technologies. It was quite an interesting experience, one I'm sure others have gone through with their own elders. I am not sure if I will find myself writing another book, but I think I can surely write *Technology 101 for Seniors!*

So much was the same, yet so much was different now. Seeing familiar faces made me feel more in sync with my surroundings. I called my life coach (a.k.a. Nagesh) to give me a massage. I was glad to see him again after two years. There were people in my mom's building to visit, like Mr. and Mrs. Bhide. When he was kind enough to escort me down from his apartment, I mentioned to Mr. Bhide that I used to play a game of jumping from the same stairs during my childhood. Now I could barely climb them with my cane. I also spoke to my badminton coach Godse Sir. (In India, folks call bosses, coaches, and the like "Sir." I still call him that.)

It was great to talk with him and thank him for instilling in me the fighting spirit that I am using to face my new normal. I also made small talk with Chanda, an extremely kind and diligent lady who had been my mom's domestic help for the past ten years or so. Many people depend upon her. I joked with my mom, "Chanda is a legend. No matter where you go in this building, it seems Chanda is there." The crazy Marathi soap opera *Mazhya navryachi bayko* that I had watched intensely two years before with Sunita and Dhananjay was still playing on TV. This time my mom and I watched with the same enthusiasm. I was totally stunned to see myself still into it and asked my mom a lot of questions to fill in the two-year gap. Whether in the East or West, soap operas are designed that way: they lock you in.

Sunita took me to the Big Bazaar store at the nearby Atria Mall for some grocery shopping. I was amazed at how good the store was. It was comparable to or better than any grocery store in the West I'd been to. As on earlier visits, I saw a new India that was constantly improving despite the many socioeconomic problems and challenges it faced. At the same time, I noticed that the political and social divides that plagued my adopted country were also plaguing the country of my birth. I prayed that the two great nations I love survive this time of divisiveness and social turmoil.

Double Whammy

Scheduling my surgery was my top priority. I visited Sportsmed Mumbai and saw my friend Dr. Antya Joshi. Like two years before, it was awesome to see him again. It was also great to finally meet Shraddha, his ultra-efficient receptionist with whom I had communicated from the US. Antya referred me to his upper limb specialist, Dr. Deepak Bhatia, who confirmed the surgery diagnosis given by Dr. Avery back in Virginia. I found Dr. Bhatia to be smart, knowledgeable, and pleasant, like one of those good-looking doctors on *ER*, *Grey's Anatomy*, or *Private Practice*. He reminded me of George Clooney or Patrick Dempsey. I must admit, though, that my personal favorite was Kate Walsh who played the role of Dr. Addison Montgomery in *Private Practice*. I had been referring to the Air India flight steward Naresh as Deepak, so maybe I subconsciously knew that I was going to meet an actual Deepak sometime soon, or it could've been a total coincidence. Who knows! In any case, I had to chuckle when I heard Dr. Bhatia's first name. We set a date and found an offsite location for my surgery. Because my stroke put me in a high-risk category, the surgery needed to take place at a facility that had an ICU in case something went wrong. Fortunately, Sir H. N. Reliance Hospital in Mumbai, which is located in Mumbai's Opera House district, about forty-five minutes from my mom's place, met the criteria I needed. Dr. Bhatia had privileges there, and it was available.

I did my best to remain active as I waited for my surgery. My dizziness and headaches were at the same levels as when I had left the States. If not exactly comfortable, I was accepting of my condition and didn't let how I felt stop me from enjoying some good times with my family. I also visited the father of my friend Mak, who lived close by. Mak's mother had passed away recently, and I wanted to grieve that loss with him. They were married for over fifty years, and I wanted to make sure he was okay. For Sunita's birthday, we went to her favorite restaurant, Swati Snacks, for some delicious Indian street food. We celebrated my mom's birthday by sharing a small cake at home before going out to Aswad, her favorite place, which serves typical cuisine from our part of the world. Still, I had to be careful. I had my first fall in three years while I was trying to pick up a phone from a nearby table. Luckily, the table absorbed the fall, and I was okay. But it was a reminder that I shouldn't be complacent.

I didn't want to lose touch with my life back in the States during this time. I kept in contact with Sandy at Avalon via email. It was sweet of her to dispose of the two garbage bags I'd forgotten to throw out when I left. Sandy emailed me that the apartment was hot and asked if I wanted her to set the thermostat to a certain temperature. Avalon had recently installed a new system which controlled door locks, thermostats, and lights. The system could be controlled through an app, so I thought, "Let's see if I can use the app to adjust the temperature." Lo and behold, it looked like it worked. Here I was, 8,000 miles away from the States, controlling the thermostat in my apartment. Isn't technology wonderful! Many residents had problems with the new system, but I guess there is a positive side to everything.

I went to the hospital to register for my surgery. The building was at least fifty years old but had been taken over by the Reliance Foundation (a foundation established in 2006 by one of the biggest conglomerates in India) and upgraded into a state-of-the-art facility. I was impressed by its beautiful old architecture when I went inside. During my visit, I was reminded of the interesting mix of languages in my native country. First, I met with Dr. Snehal, the anesthesiologist who needed to approve my planned surgery. I started to speak with her in Hindi and English, then found out her last name was Kale, a name from my part of the world. Once I knew that, we started to converse in Marathi. In India, you can usually tell by someone's last name what region they are from and what language they may speak. Second, I assumed the same about Dr. Bhatia, whose last name indicated to me that he was from the north of India and spoke Hindi. I was conversing in Hindi and English with him, but later found out that he had grown up in Mumbai and speaks fluent Marathi, so we switched to Marathi. This is a common pattern in my native country. Most Indians start a conversation in Hindi or English and then switch to the regional language if it is familiar to both speakers. (In the States, I don't believe we can tell where someone is from based on their last name.) Last, I was totally startled to hear an American-sounding voice announcing the number for people waiting in the registration area of the hospital.

This was certainly not an accent I was used to in India. I thought to myself, "What the heck is an American doing here?" It took me a moment to realize that it was probably the standard voice of an automated system the hospital had purchased from the US.

The night before my surgery, I checked into the hospital. Sunita was kind enough to stay overnight with me. It was my first hospital stay since I'd been released from Inova Mount Vernon in March 2017. I felt anxious as things got underway, but Dr. Bhatia's presence calmed me down. When I saw how he directed the operating room procedures, I could only think of the focus and sense of control that Stephen Strasburg shows as the ace pitcher for the Washington Nationals. I could see how much respect the entire operating staff had for Dr. Bhatia. I knew I was in good hands.

After the hour-and-a-half surgery, Dr. Bhatia met with me along with Sunita and Dhananjay. He told us that he had not only successfully repaired my rotator cuff but also my bicep. I felt grateful to the entire hospital staff for the excellent care they had given me. As in Nimba, the staff was diverse, reflecting India's different regions and religions. Besides Dr. Bhatia, I was impressed by medical resident fellow Sana Sheikh from Mumbai, and especially the medical technician, Sikander, a young lad who was Jai's age and from the north Indian state of Jharkhand. In conversation, I found out that Sikander, at his young age, was sending money to his family, as he wanted to contribute to getting his sister married. He was happy to work at Sir H. N. Reliance, but was hoping to get a higher paying job, maybe overseas.

Something about the kid made me want to help him. I told him that I would help him network once I returned to the States. It was one way I could give back for the excellent care he and his colleagues had given me.

I noticed that Sir H. N. Reliance had similar challenges to what I had seen at Nimba and Inova Mount Vernon Hospital. My belief was confirmed that most challenges faced by businesses are process and communication related and not people related, whether in the East or West. Even though the hospital stay was only for three days, I could not wait to go home to my mom's.

I went home with my right arm in a sling, happy that the surgery was a success but knowing that I would have to manage with my weak left arm for at least six weeks. I told myself, "At least you have your left hand. Some people don't even have that luxury." Still, it was a double whammy to have my good arm in a sling while relying on my weakened left arm and hand for everyday tasks. It was difficult, but I learned to cope. It proved especially challenging to brush my teeth, drink coffee (I used a straw), read a newspaper, and sleep (I did it upright with a backrest as Dr. Bhatia had recommended). I was able to feed myself by taking a piece of roti, filling it with a combination of dried vegetables, chutneys, jams, or pickles, and rolling it up like a taco. Anything that was liquid, my mom would feed me.

Jugaad

Dealing with my limitations taught me lessons in *jugaad*, a Hindi word defined by Wikipedia as "a non-conventional, frugal innovation." Jugaad is comparable to a "hack" in American slang. Indians are masters of jugaad: they learn how to work with breakdowns in systems or processes that crop up in everyday life, often making up the solutions as they go along with whatever materials are handy. My mom is adept at jugaad; maybe some of her skill has rubbed off on me. I noticed the other day that Mom was watching a movie called *Jugaad*. I chuckled at that and teased her by calling her the Queen of Jugaad. Those who know her will agree with this description.

After my surgery, I kept reminding myself that "it is what it is." I did my best to stay calm and not get frustrated. My countdown to the day the sling would come off (at that point April 9) had begun in earnest. In the meantime, I had to rely on Mom for help with nearly everything. I told her, "I feel like I am in kindergarten again." I couldn't feed myself, pick up my clothes, comb my hair, or shave. I joked with her that she was my quasi nurse-cook-personal aide-psychologist all in one.

But I was glad I came to stay with Mom. There was no way I could've managed on my own in Virginia. Although my capacity was dramatically reduced, I did feel lucky that I had sensation in my right hand. Even with the sling on, I could use my laptop as well as give voice commands. Being able to keep working on *One Fine Day* made me feel extremely proud and happy. I also continued to keep myself busy as much as I could: paying bills online, keeping up with some paperwork, and updating the project plan for my book (yes, I had a project plan for the book). I continued using WhatsApp messaging to communicate with folks instead of calling. Talking on the phone gave me more headaches, and I preferred to use messaging—it was counterintuitive for sure.

President Trump came for a two-day state visit to India. It's interesting that in my hallucinations after my brain surgeries, I was in Mumbai with President Trump. Now he was actually in India for a state visit when I was here. Of course I was not with him, but I enthusiastically watched his visit on TV. I wished I were with the president, like I was in my hallucination.

Through it all, part of me kept hoping that a magic pill could be found. I started to think that once I got back home, I would explore how to get into clinical trials—there was always the possibility of a cure, no matter how small. Meanwhile, old friends continued to come back into my life. Neighbors from mom's building whom I'd known since my childhood stopped by, as well as school and college friends.

Talking with people from my past felt good. I especially liked discussing my book with Mr. Bhide, an avid reader. Old friends and neighbors were interested in how I was coping during my recovery. I told them, "I am spending quality time with my mamma."

There were more positive developments and challenges. I hired a home aide named Anand to take some of the care burden from my mom. He was a young, sincere guy who worked multiple jobs to provide for his family. He reminded me of my home aide Pearl in Virginia and my attendant Vinubhai at Nimba. I also had a barber pay me a home visit to give me a haircut, just as I had done two years before. These were everyday things I could do for myself.

There were always new complications to deal with. My mom was diagnosed with a common medical issue in seniors. Her symptoms were not severe but still raised concern. She needed surgery as soon as possible, but we did not want to schedule until after my sling came off. Her doctor agreed to wait as long as her symptoms did not worsen.

Life continued in the streets of Mumbai all around us. I noticed a lot of change as I had two years before. Mostly they were good, though with development also comes some unwanted things. But the more things changed, the more they stayed the same too. I could hear the same merchants shouting for customers below our window as I had growing up, one who ran a utensils exchange business, the other who sharpened kitchen knives. The janitor in my mom's apartment building was the same lady who was there when I was young. A worshipper of the Hindu goddess Kadak Lakshmi visited our street to beg for money while whipping himself (those who follow this goddess believe the goddess protects them). A recycler came by my mom's apartment every month or so to collect, weigh, and purchase her old newspapers. This system is common in India. He was the son of the recycler who used to come when I was a boy. These and other familiar characters reminded me how much Mumbai had stayed the same even in the face of the enormous changes the city and India had seen since my childhood.

My dizziness, headaches, and balance issues were the same as when I'd left Virginia. I was starting to feel that these conditions could be permanent. They remained the one constant factor in my new normal. But "it is what it is" remained my mantra as I reminded myself that I had come a long way over the past three years.

The World's New Normal

As coronavirus cases grew across the globe in early March, I could not help but think that the world itself was facing its one fine day and its resulting new normal. In my case, that meant facing a whole new set of restrictions on top of having my arm in the sling. I made sure I washed my hands regularly, refrained from shaking hands or giving hugs, and stopped ordering food from outside. I made sure Anand washed his hands when he came over. When I left the US in early February, I never could have expected that this pandemic would've had such a dramatic effect on the entire world. I would not have been able to travel if I had waited until later.

After the surgery, I spent fourteen days straight in the apartment without going out. It was difficult to walk down the two flights of stairs with a sling on my good arm until

Dr. Bhatia removed my stiches. This was the longest I had gone without going out due to my health. Back in Virginia, there were many times (two to three days) when I could not go out due to dizziness and headaches. Although extremely frustrating, it was the most prudent thing to do in my recovery journey. Although I was on track with my recovery and feeling less pain, I was still anxious for the sling to come off.

The fourth week after surgery found me longing to get out of the apartment. I was determined not to be home that long without going out. So I was happy when Sunita and Dhananjay offered to take me for a ride around Mumbai. We went on the Bandra-Worli Sea Link, a cable-stayed bridge that crosses Mahim Bay and offers a superb view of the city. The bridge reminded me of the Zakim Bunker Hill Memorial Bridge in Boston. Seeing downtown Mumbai from the Sea Link reminded me of how the New York City skyline looks from one of the bridges there. The sight was beautiful, but it was eerie too. Because of the coronavirus, the hustle and bustle of the Mumbai streets was gone. The Lord Ganesh Siddhivinayak Temple was closed to the public for the first time in 200 years. It was heartbreaking to see coronavirus casualties increasing and triggering economic meltdowns back home and around the world. On March 16, the Dow Jones index suffered its single biggest day drop ever; India's equivalent, Sensex, suffered a massive decline as well. The world was indeed having its one fine day—the unfortunate kind—and facing a new normal no one could have expected.

I knew that we all had to accept and embrace this new normal, no matter how hard it was. There were no magic pills within reach, no easy answers to fall back on. This was true on both an individual and global level.

Unfortunately, my dizziness, headache, and balance issues spiked once again. Since I had to be helped down the stairs and avoided going out, I saw my situation as a "self-quarantine by default." But I did witness something amazing, which I will never forget. At the urging of Prime Minister Narendra Modi, Indians observed a total "people's curfew" one day. The entire country of 1.3 billion people completely shut down voluntarily. It was certainly eerie, to see a megalopolis like Mumbai so quiet. Another fascinating sight was the many people who came out in droves on balconies and patios in the evening for five to ten minutes and clapped and made sounds to thank the medical staffs, the police, and other folks who were working around the clock to fight the coronavirus.

I told my loved ones, "Hang in there. This will also pass at some point, though we don't know when. Until then, we just have to hunker down." I thought of the World Champion Washington Nationals manager, Davey Martinez's mantra: "Let's Go 1–0." Keep moving ahead one win at a time and don't think about the entire season or the record.

Things got even more serious on March 24 when India announced a twenty-one-day lockdown across the entire country. It was not an easy thing to order in a country of 1.3 billion people, but given the gravity of the situation, it was necessary. India was confronting the situation on a war footing, and the country was taking steps to slow down the spread of the coronavirus. On a personal level, it meant that my new normal changed once again. Anand would not be coming by to help me with shaving and bathing, and my sling would not come off for a few more days. We had to delay Mom's surgery, as it was an elective procedure, and we were rightly advised to wait until the lockdown was eased.

I was back into kindergarten mode with my mom giving me sponge baths. I could not shave, so I grew a beard, like I had right after my stroke. Like many other people, it was my lockdown look.

Thank God my mom and I had each other during the lockdown. I continued to teach her how to use different technologies effectively and had interesting conversations with her on a variety of topics. Sports was an interest we shared. She doesn't understand anything about American football, but that didn't stop her from discussing it. She loves wide receiver DeSean Jackson's explosive style of play because she had seen him go on a rampage for the Washington Redskins on TV during her last visit to the States in 2016. Mom is an avid tennis fan and missed watching the French Open after it was canceled. Marathi and Hindi music were other fun topics for us. She is obsessed with singing and has a good voice. We did have some respectful disagreements on Indian local and national politics where I dared to differ with her on her strong views with my independent thinking. We discussed many things, but two conversations stand out to me: how the pandemic would change life in India and around the world, and explaining to her the US Electoral College system during elections. She was totally confused by it and not able to understand it.

After my futile attempts, I let it go and changed the topic. I hope I can explain it to her sometime in the future. Because of the lockdown, there were no new episodes of *Mazhya navryachi bayko*. So we regularly watched reruns of one of India's popular TV series, *The Mahabharata*, an ancient epic. Beyond this, there were things we shared about each other's lives that we wouldn't have normally discussed. I can't say we learned a lot of new things about each other, since we know one another so well, but I did find out how talented a poet she is in Marathi. She wrote some beautiful poetry on different topics like the effects of the corona pandemic on us, how life as a senior citizen is challenging, and, my favorite—written about *moi*—titled "My Son." It rhymes beautifully in Marathi, and brought tears to my eyes. Here is a rough translation.

> *My son, didn't think you will write a book, but anything is possible in this world.*
>
> *My son, you have come back from the grip of death and have stood firmly.*
>
> *My son, I am stunned to see your self-confidence and willpower and choke with emotion.*
>
> *My son, I am always behind you. Face all the challenges without getting disappointed and shaken.*
>
> *My son, I am praying to God, please give my son the strength to live, my faith in you will automatically increase.*

It was great to be able to have these conversations. I chuckled when I read somewhere, "India is the country with highest per capita opinion." How true! Being from here, I knew that before, but certainly noticed it more now and during my last trips to Mumbai and Nimba.

But not everything was always hunky-dory. There were a few times when my mom and I got on each other's nerves, such as when she kept asking me about the process of writing *One Fine Day* or about technology. My repeated questions about her buying new gadgets or appliances for her apartment were irritating her. It's not surprising there would be a little static between us after so much time together in this lockdown, as I'm sure it was in many other families. But overall, we got along simply fine. We would also talk with Sunita and Dhananjay at least once a day by phone, and later, via video calls. They would come to see us occasionally to deliver medicine, groceries, and other items.

Let's Go 1-0!

My concerns about the pandemic continued to grow. News reports about the numbers of coronavirus casualties back home were frightening. I was totally stunned to hear those reports and kept thinking, "This does not happen to the United States. It happens elsewhere." How wrong I was, unfortunately. I felt incredibly sad and was worried about Monica and the boys, who were under a statewide stay-at-home order. India, like the US, was on edge, expecting the infection to peak over the next two weeks. I prayed every day for the two countries. I started to think I wouldn't be able to return home before July or August. Luckily, I had my mom and sister here in case I needed to extend my stay. Not only was I facing this new normal with the lockdown, but my headache and dizziness spiked once again, hurting my surgery incision point as it had before. Instead of getting frustrated and pissed, I focused on what I could do to alleviate the spike. I took some Advil, and my mom gave me a scalp massage with oil, followed by a sponge bath. That same week, I started to sniffle and had some throat irritation. I worried that these might be symptoms of the coronavirus infection. "That's the last thing I need," I thought. Fortunately, it turned out I only had an old-fashioned cold, as the weather had started to change in Mumbai. My mom swung into action and made me inhale steam vapor, and gargle with warm water and turmeric. Indians are in love with turmeric, and they believe it is a natural antiseptic, among having other beneficial qualities.

The lockdown really brought out my mom's jugaad skills. When I lost network connectivity to the 4G dongle device we had, Dhananjay offered me his. I would have been pissed off by this a few years earlier, but now I was definitely calmer, as I kept reminding myself "it is what it is." I tried for an hour, but it just wouldn't work. My mom swung into action and somehow got it to start. She truly lived up to her title the Queen of Jugaad!

I enjoyed teasing and joking with my mom, but I also could not help feeling bad for her. There was no help available due to the lockdown, so she had to do everything herself:

cooking, washing dishes, laundry, dusting, cleaning, and more. This was in addition to taking care of me. I could not help but think about how after my stroke I was totally dependent on Monica for a few months, and now I was totally dependent on my mom—of course for different reasons, but still totally dependent. But there was nothing I could have done then or now.

I was more anxious than ever for my sling to come off, but that was now delayed until April 15 at the earliest. All I could do was remain calm. I had been in Mumbai for two months. Ideally, I had two months to go before returning home, but I had my doubts I would be returning to the States that soon. The temperatures and humidity in Mumbai rose, and I was reminded of the upcoming, brutal summer days of April and May, before the rainy season starts in June, and it cools down a little bit. But there was no escaping the high humidity, as Mumbai is on the coast of the Arabian Sea.

More grim news continued to pour in: coronavirus deaths back home had reached the 23,000 mark. Although not as dire as in the States, India's total cases of infection and deaths rose as well. I kept hearing the word *intubation* in connection with the crisis. I knew exactly what it meant, because I too had undergone this medical procedure during my stay at Inova Fairfax Hospital. As I'd anticipated, around Easter time, India extended the nationwide lockdown by two more weeks. Lockdown 2.0 had started, and a new countdown started for me—for the lockdown to end. I kept repeating Davey Martinez's mantra, "Let's go 1–0" to keep my spirit up. My mom had no idea who the heck Davey

Martinez was, so I explained the gist of who he was and what he meant.

Seven weeks in a sling was starting to feel like enough. I told Dr. Bhatia that it was impossible for me to continue with my right hand immobile for two more weeks. He agreed that we could remove the sling and start the rehab process. He referred me to Rupali, a highly experienced therapist he had worked with for several years. I started rehab sessions with her over video calls. This was turning into an Offshore 3.0 rehab visit, but of course for different reasons. Rupali told me that I would slowly but surely increase mobility in my arm but advised me to wear the sling while sleeping for the next two weeks. She added that I could gradually stop using the backrest when I slept. She gave me a pair of daily exercises to do, one in the morning and one at night, and we agreed to do a video call each week. Now, besides my remote meditation sessions with Sagar—who now was no longer with Nimba but in the southern city of Chennai—I was doing rehab consultations via video. With lockdowns in effect across the globe, people were turning to similar remote technologies to work, study, and entertain themselves. It was a new normal for me, like the rest of the world.

We all had to find ways to deal with the crisis. Through social media, I learned that my old college friend Mahalaxmi Iyer, a popular Bollywood singer, was taking part in a living room concert for fans via Zoom and Facebook. The concert was organized to raise money for a national trust fund established by India's prime minister to aid those affected by the coronavirus pandemic or other calamities. I loved the concert's tagline: "Socially Distant, Digitally Close." How appropriate for the times! I knew Mahalaxmi through Vrinda, as they were close friends. She and I had stayed in touch a little even after she became a famous singer. Fame hadn't changed her. She was still the humble, down-to-earth person I'd known when we were both in college.

I finally ate dinner with my right hand for the first time in seven weeks. When my mom started to feed me out of habit, I gently reminded her that I could now feed myself. It was a funny and cute moment we shared. I started calling my timeline BS (before sling) and AS (after sling).

My mom found the lockdown extension challenging, even though she knew it made sense. For my part, I felt concerned for the parents of many of my friends back in the States and checked in on them when I could. It also saddened me to think that my plans to meet with many friends before I left to go back home looked so improbable now. Although I knew the physical lockdown was necessary, like so many other people, I worried about the consequences of the "emotional lockdown" the whole world was experiencing. We were witnessing unprecedented deaths and suffering around the world, and I knew that would bring extreme sadness and depression to many for a long time. I thought about the first responders and frontline workers around the world. They were the heroes in this crisis. Besides those heroes, I thought kids were also the real heroes. Schools had shut down, there were no extracurricular activities, and many kids were stressed and feeling isolated, but found ways to adapt to this new normal, and this was quite inspiring to me. And I believed a silver lining would be found in the resulting new normal the pandemic would create. The potential was there for many people to reevaluate their lives and make some positive changes. It reminded me of the lyrics to my favorite Michael Jackson song "Man in the Mirror." It was up to all of us to change ourselves first and then transform the world.

At the suggestion of my friend Aimee back in the States, I watched a live stream of Pope Francis delivering his Easter Sunday sermon in an empty Vatican City. I agreed with Aimee that watching the papal mass in an almost empty St. Peter's Basilica and Square was watching living history. Even though I am not a Christian, I wanted to watch the moment unfold and hear the pope's prayers for the world. We were all in this together. I found the pope's comments to reporters meaningful: "Be messengers of life in a time of death. . . . We have to respond to our confinement with all our creativity. We can either get depressed and alienated . . . or we can get creative. . . . To be in lockdown but yearning, with that memory that yearns and begets hope, this is what will help us escape our confinement." These words resonated with me. He also said that deep spiritual introspection will be needed as the world settles into its post-pandemic new normal. "Absolutely! Right on!" I thought. What he said about how we should deal with the pandemic is also so true, how we should respond to any life changes and its resulting new normal, no matter what they are.

Life went on. Sunita came over to drop off some medicines she'd picked up at the chemist for me and Mom. It made me happy to see her after so many days apart. She also brought some delicious food she had cooked—a change for her. Even though she is talented in the kitchen, she normally prefers to have her cook, Meena, prepare meals. When Meena was prevented from coming over because of the lockdown, Sunita started to cook more often. I am sure Dhananjay would agree with me that although the lockdown was challenging, there were some unexpected benefits! I believe many folks around the world were in this boat: they started to cook more at home.

As I completed one week of rehab exercises, I felt good overall. The exercises were not that difficult, though my right arm did hurt a bit. Dr. Bhatia had told me I still had about three to four months of rehab before I could use my arm and hand normally. Slow and steady progress was what I needed to maintain.

Keeping positive during this time wasn't always easy. I was pained to see when the death count back home crossed the 40,000 mark. Like many, I just could not believe this was happening in our United States, especially when there were not many cases and no deaths when I left in early February. At the same time, I was learning to accept that my dizziness, headache, and balance issues were going to be a permanent part of my new normal. The levels of these symptoms were clearly higher than when I'd come to India. As frustrating as it was, the only way I could accept this reality was to keep reminding myself that "it is what it is," and at least I was alive now, and it had been almost over three and a half years ago that I'd had my stroke. Where I was now would be my new baseline. If the levels of these issues came down a bit, that would purely be a bonus.

I started doing two more rehab exercises with Rupali. The pain in my arm increased, so she advised me to put ice on it and take one or two days off from exercising. Enduring all this discomfort made me think about karma (actions), the belief many Indians have that what happens to you in life is the result of good or bad karma. Some people believe your karma has no effect on this life, but does affect the next life. I am not a big believer in that thought process, but like when I had seen Mr. Pancholi (the astrologer) during my last trip, I went with the flow. I joked with my mom that perhaps the kind of dramatic life changes I had faced over the last three years were because in my past life I may have killed someone, and I was now paying the price in this life. With the elevated dizziness, headache, and balance issues and now this throbbing arm pain, I joked further with her that it might mean not only that I may have killed someone in my last life, but that I also may have been a serial killer. I didn't really believe that, but who the hell knows!

Looking Beyond the Lockdown

My belief in humanity was confirmed again with an incredible incident. I sent money through PayPal to Amy, my book cover designer back in the States. In error, however, I actually sent it to another Amy, whose email address was quite similar. When I realized my mistake and contacted the

Amy who I had sent the money to in error, requesting she send the money back, she did so instantly. I was blown away by her honesty and promptness. I knew she was somewhere in the States, but I had no idea who she was or where exactly she was. I truly appreciated her honesty. Not only didn't we know each other, I was also 8,000 miles away.

I kept busy by helping my mom's neighbor and friend Mrs. Junnarkar with a technology problem. I'd known her since I was a child, and I could not help but notice that she had the exact same questions and challenges as my mom. The idea of writing *Technology 101 for Seniors* gained momentum in my mind. But such worthwhile distractions didn't stop me from realizing that I had been cooped up in Mom's apartment for thirty days straight. The lockdown had controlled the spread of the virus in India, but cases were still slowly creeping up. It was becoming clear that I wouldn't be able to go outside anytime soon. I needed patience more than ever.

My recovery from surgery found me counting down the days until the lockdown ended. I resumed my rehab exercises but was careful to do no harm. I kept my temper in check even when the only air-conditioning unit in the apartment stopped working. In India, generally, there is no central air-conditioning, but some apartments have room air-conditioners. Due to the lockdown, my mom's regular repair person could not come, so we tried to find someone else. Even though I had grown up in Mumbai without air-conditioning, I wasn't ready to endure the scorching summer heat and humidity now. Though my sense of "it is what it is" was tested big time, I managed to stay relatively calm. Looking at my plight, the Queen of Jugaad swung into action once again. She clicked all the buttons many times, and miraculously the air-conditioner started working. Jugaad saved me one more time. Later on, I was able to finally convince my mom to get an air-conditioner for the living room—something Sunita, Dhananjay, and I had tried over the last twenty years to convince my mom and dad to do.

There was no jugaad-like fix for my right arm, however. It continued to hurt, so Rupali advised that I avoid even limited use of it. Now I was forced back into kindergarten mode, which was very frustrating. For over a month, my aging mom had to do all the chores in the apartment, in addition to taking care of me. Though she didn't complain, I'm sure it was taxing for her. Since I couldn't be of much help, we decided to ask Chanda to come back to work. Of course, we asked her to adhere to strict social distancing guidelines while performing her tasks. Unfortunately, the same wasn't possible in the case of Anand, my home care aide. Nor could I call my life coach to come. Once again, what could I say except "it is what it is."

As the end of April approached, I continued to be stunned and horrified by the course of the virus. In India, the number of infections continued to rise, although luckily, it was low compared with some other countries. Prime Minister Modi extended the lockdown for another two weeks. Lockdown 3.0 had started.

The entire country was classified into one of three zones: red, yellow, or green with some restrictions eased in certain zones. India had done a decent job at the front end to lockdown the country early in the pandemic, but as the country started to slowly reopen, the cases started to increase.

I tried to keep in touch with the outside world and share what was positive with those I cared about. I keenly followed the NFL college draft picks online. Jai and I exchanged happy texts about the Washington Redskins drafting Chase Young as an edge rusher. I noted with pleasure that Mahalaxmi offered another living room concert—this time solo, on Facebook Live. As usual, she was brilliant. There were sadder moments as well. Like so many others in India, I mourned the deaths of two Bollywood megastars to cancer—Rishi Kapoor and Irfan Khan. RIP.

We tentatively scheduled Mom's surgery for when we thought the lockdown might be lifted. I tried to keep Davey Martinez's determination in mind, while staying realistic about the struggles ahead. Nobody said the new normal would be easy, or even possible to predict. But we had no choice but to move forward.

• • •

"Optimism is the faith that leads to achievement. Nothing can be done without hope and confidence."

—HELEN KELLER

Health Recovery Level

Stall in recovery
continues.

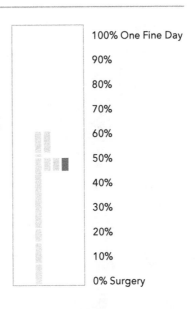

100% One Fine Day

90%

80%

70%

60%

50%

40%

30%

20%

10%

0% Surgery

SAMEERISM • Whatever life change you are facing, physical or emotional, *only you* can determine if you can participate in certain activities. Listen to your heart and mind. Sometimes the heart wins over the mind; sometimes it's the other way around. The bottom line is that only you can make the call. Listen to your body and go with what feels right for *you*. Other people mean well with their suggestions, but only you can decide what things you can do.

CHAPTER 11

Hope for
the Future

"Once you choose hope, anything is possible."

CHRISTOPHER REEVE

As I started a new countdown for Lockdown 3.0 to end, I took stock of what I had been through and what was still ahead for me. I was nearing the three-month mark of my visit to Mumbai, a trip that had lasted far longer than I had expected. So many things had happened during this time, not only for me but also the world at large. Staying in place encourages you to think about what is really important in life. Among other things, I realized what unconditional love is all about. Spending three months with my mom made me fully realize her unconditional love for me. I think most of the moms all over the world feel this way toward their children. If I can express even half of that to my loved ones, I will consider myself very lucky.

Slowly and cautiously, people were venturing back out again. I was happy that Chanda had come back to help Mom around the apartment. She followed strict social distancing protocols. At the same time, as with many people, video calls and other forms of technology were helping me stay connected. Besides doing remote meditation sessions with Sagar in Chennai and tele-rehab with Rupali in Mumbai, I was now doing remote sessions with my clinical psychologist, Dr. Susan, back home. I mentioned to her that talking to patients through video calls might be her post-pandemic new normal. I knew this was not totally comfortable for her due to the privacy and security issues involved, a concern I am sure many other doctors also shared.

I understood Dr. Susan's hesitation, but I think there is no choice but for doctors to find innovative and different ways to practice their craft remotely rather than always see their patients face-to-face. This applies not just to doctors but to all service providers. I also had some other non-brain related medical issue, and I did a tele-consult with Dr. Pathare, even though his practice was only a few blocks away from my mom's apartment. Whether a provider was nearby or thousands of miles away, this was going to be the new normal. Even my mom did her consult via a video call with her doctor, complete with audio through my AirPods. I think my technology training was yielding results. She passed the "test" with flying colors. She had never done a video consult before. *Technology 101 for Seniors*, here I come.

High Touch or High Tech

Years ago, I had encouraged one of the organizations I worked for to use technology to enhance customer experience. I used to say, "I want to transform the company from being high touch to high tech." There is nothing wrong with being high touch, but technology used correctly can be effective for businesses and individuals. This can be especially true for people with physical challenges. I have used so many tools and practices to make my life easier: video calls using Facetime, Zoom, or WhatsApp; remote meditation sessions via Skype or WhatsApp; text messages on WhatsApp and Facebook Messenger; larger fonts and speech recognition programs on my laptop; and much more. Through these platforms and apps, I could stay connected with friends, family members, and the outside world in general. Technology allows people with ongoing medical or physical issues to fit in and integrate with the rest of society; otherwise they can feel very isolated. I have seen the good it can do firsthand.

Thanks to FaceTime and WhatsApp, I stayed in regular touch with Jai and Arjun. Like most kids in the world, they were fighting the boredom of being home while taking online classes and waiting for stay-at-home orders or lockdowns to end. They were understandably worried about the pandemic and the recent outbreak of violence at protests across the country to combat racial injustice, but they were not frightened. I was glad to see them staying strong in the face of so much disturbing news, just as they had when I was recovering at Inova Mount Vernon. I wondered if this would be the new normal for them—and for us all.

There were lessons to be learned in how different people faced this uncertain time. I read how Amma, the Hindu spiritual leader known as the hugging saint, was facing her own new normal. Amma was famous for giving her followers a tight embrace to help alleviate their problems. Over the last forty years or so, she had hugged more than 30 million people worldwide. Now, she had to stop due to the pandemic. I liked what she said about this unfortunate situation: "While analyzing time, you realize that nothing really exists other than the present moment. Planning is important, but we have to know how to adapt and adjust when our plans fail. Detachment doesn't mean disinterest or lack of caring; it means acceptance of whatever comes, understanding that we are not in control of that." Those words were appropriate and inspiring. I kept what Amma said in mind as I navigated my new normal. I think the whole world would benefit from her sense of acceptance as well.

My dizziness, headache, and balance issues spiked to a new level. It was very frustrating to deal with, but I kept reminding myself, "It is what it is." I decided that whenever the lockdown was lifted, I would have a CAT scan done to make sure there was no new bleeding or other unexpected symptoms, just as I had done back home. This was something that was constantly on my mind: to get a CAT scan and pray there was nothing new.

Anniversaries and Inspirations

On Mother's Day, I felt blessed to celebrate the day with my mom. Even though we could not take her out due to the lockdown, it was nice to just be with her. Mom continued to help me take care of myself in whatever ways she could. After Anand stopped coming to the apartment when the lockdown began, Mom began giving me sponge baths. Taking a shower by myself was not an option, as I was still recovering from my surgery, and the floor in the bathroom was quite slippery. Finally, Mom became the Queen of Jugaad once again and enabled me to take a shower after almost fifty days without one. She spread bathmats and towels on the floor so I wouldn't slip, and adjusted the water temperature and position of the showerhead for me. Only she could do those things, as the fixtures were old. It truly felt awesome and rejuvenating to take a shower once again.

The Queen of Jugaad did two more things for me. I needed loose-fitting shirts as I recovered from my surgery. I constantly wore the one shirt I had that wasn't tight. Since I could not order a new shirt online due to the lockdown, my mom tapped into her jugaad mind and stitched me a shirt made from one of her old nightgowns. Now I had a second loose-fitting shirt with a lady's nightgown look to it. Because it was no longer possible to go to a barber or have one come to the apartment, Mom trimmed my hair a little using my razor. All the hacks worked, and she delivered once again.

The eighth anniversary of my father's death was a somber one, especially since Mom and I were together in the same apartment. I still remember the day when he passed away in my arms. I had flown to Mumbai that day and arrived only six or seven hours before his passing. I was extremely lucky and grateful to God for the opportunity to spend a few hours with him. Even after so many years, we still missed him terribly, though we know that he is in a good place. I have many great memories of the times we spent together. For years, my father would wake up at 5:30 a.m. and take me to badminton training or swimming lessons. I can still see him sitting at his computer table or playing *carrom* (an Indian board game) in our living room or using his electric razor. I am sure the noise from my electric razor reminded my mom of my father. My father and mother were married for forty-eight years. Although she is very strong, I could see the pain in my mom's eyes on that sad anniversary. She cooked some of my father's favorite foods for us that day. She used to always make him fruit salad with yogurt and cauliflower curry on his birthday. I am truly blessed to have had good parents while growing up. I believe I have developed strength and whatever creativity I have from my mother and independent thinking and practicality from my father. Some of it is genetic, some of it learned.

Being a very gentle person, my father would have found it extremely hard to watch his son go through these adversities. But I know he would have been proud of me for the way I have faced them and for my determination to write *One Fine Day*.

The fear of the pandemic continued in India and back

home. I heard about the first confirmed case of coronavirus at Avalon. Meanwhile, I worried once again that I might have contracted COVID-19. Mom and I kept a sharp eye out for any symptoms specific to the virus. Luckily, what I had was just another small cold. Once again, I gargled with turmeric and inhaled vapor to feel better.

Remote sessions remained important as the lockdown dragged on. I continued with my tele-session schedule: meditation with Sagar, rehab with Rupali, counseling with Dr. Susan, and keeping in touch with folks who were helping me write *One Fine Day*. I read in a Marathi newspaper what Dr. Yash Velankar wrote: "I am not a slave of my brain, I am its master." I guess this is what Sagar and Dr. Susan have meant over the past three years.

I tried to keep in touch with as many friends as I could. Among them was Antya, who told me about his recent bicycle trips and races all over India and the rest of the world. I told him that his being so fit and active in his sixties was a true inspiration to me.

Against All Odds, I Am Fighting

On May 31, the lockdown across India was extended again by two more weeks. Lockdown 4.0 had begun. Those states in the yellow and green zones had many of their restrictions eased. Mumbai was still in the red zone, so only a few restrictions were eased. I hadn't been outside my mom's apartment since Sunita and Dhananjay had taken me for a ride in late March.

I finally ventured out for my three-month ultrasound checkup at Sportsmed, as well as another appointment for a CAT scan. The ultrasound was done by an extremely efficient and pleasant lady, Dr. Ankita Ahuja, and showed that my shoulder was healing well, though it was going to take several more months for me to resume some normal functions. Dr. Bhatia advised me to move to the next level of rehab. These trips were essential, though not exactly pleasant. I was dealing with my dizziness, headache, and balance issues, wearing a face mask and disposable gloves in the hot Mumbai summer. Even so, it was worth the discomfort to be outside after two months of confinement.

Like the last few times, my CAT scan revealed no new bleeding. I was concerned, though, that a buildup of fluid was detected in my cerebellum. I mailed the report to Kedar's cousin Dr. Pradyumna Oak, head of neurology at Nanavati Hospital, one of the Mumbai region's top medical facilities. I had met Dr. Oak when he had visited Kedar and Vrinda in New Jersey. He had impressed me as brilliant and highly capable. Informally, I also showed it to Dr. Svet Djurkovic (Dr. D.) back home at Fairfax Inova Hospital, whom I had stayed in touch with since he'd treated me in the ICU. They both agreed that the report looked okay. I decided to see Dr. Oak after the lockdown was lifted to learn if he had any recommendations to address my ongoing issues. I was secretly hoping he would have the magic pill I had been searching for these past three and a half years. I knew that the chances of finding a magical cure were slim, but the hope was still there. When Anil had faced many adversities over the years, he used to say, "Against all the odds, I am fighting." Now this was my mantra.

My dizziness and headache (especially the latter) spiked once again. The area around the incision point was throbbing. Even though I knew the CAT scan was clear, I was worried. I made a video appointment with Dr. Oak to get his opinion. Like other doctors and neurologists in India and back home, he said the CAT scan was fine but could not explain the spike. He did not have that magic pill. It was a hard thing to accept that these issues may be permanent and may or may not diminish over time, but with my "never give up" and "try everything" philosophy, I decided to continue trying different therapies and treatments to see if they might help. My philosophy still was, "if it is not going to kill me, let's try it." Enrolling in a clinical trial for my issues when I got back home remained a goal. For the present, I had to miss my rehab sessions, though I was able to do another video consult with Dr. Pathare.

Heartache and Hard Rain

I was deeply saddened to learn that the US hit the grim milestone of 100,000 deaths due to COVID-19. It also broke my heart to see the events in Minneapolis, and I felt equally sad about the looting and burning that happened in that city and many others. I had thought these things happened in other countries, but not in our country. It was surreal. It was like someone had cast an evil eye on my country. I prayed for our country to heal from this.

Many people I spoke with in India were stunned, too, but could not fully understand what was happening in the States. I tried to put the racial injustice issue into an Indian context. In India, it's not a Black and white issue, but rather an upper and lower caste one. Although the issues facing both countries are not exactly comparable, there are many similarities between these ongoing conflicts. But just as I am hopeful for my future, I also strongly believe we, as a country, have hope for the nation on this very issue. There is no doubt this is causing a lot of pain, anger, and frustration. The issue has to be addressed for sure, but we all have to remember that we have come a long way and will continue to make progress no matter how slow or frustrating it may be. Even though I was hopeful about the future, these events disturbed me so much I requested that Sagar do a remote meditation session with me. It definitely helped me to calm down.

By early June, restrictions were lifted in most of the lockdown areas. But the authorities had identified containment zones for which the lockdown continued. As the country started to slowly reopen—the government called it Unlock 1.0—most people understood that they had to be careful and patient. Also, no one was sure what the approaching intense monsoon season would bring.

Because international flights in India had not resumed yet, I needed to postpone my return plans for later in the summer. But United Airlines was not accepting any rescheduling requests at that point. Even though I was with my family, I missed my life back home terribly. I could not wait to resume it. I was anxious and sad that I wasn't able to return to the States after nearly four months in India. But I knew I was in the high-risk category to contract the coronavirus and that flying back under those conditions was dangerous. I reminded myself once again that "it is what it is" and thought that, since my family had not been able to be with me for my fiftieth birthday last year, God had given me the opportunity to be with them this year.

The first monsoon rains came to Mumbai. They relieved some of the heat and mugginess the city had been experiencing for several months, but they were also a reminder of the fury they could bring for the next two to three months. The ferocious monsoon rains are critical for India, not just for the agriculture-dependent economy, but also for the whole economy in general. Good agricultural production leads to increased demand for consumer goods, which helps the economy grow. Although essential, monsoons are violent weather systems, which bring heavy rainfall resulting in waterlogging, property damage, and other challenges. This was going to be my first full monsoon season in thirty years.

Besides the coronavirus pandemic and the upcoming monsoon, Mumbai was also hit with a rare cyclone. The last time that happened was seventy-two years ago. Like my ever-changing new normal, the maximum city's new normal was changing as well. Luckily, the city was spared the brunt of the storm.

In the middle of all this, my thoughts were never far away from home. It felt great to stay involved with Fairfax Inova's Patient and Family Advisory Council. It met for the first time via Zoom after its last few meetings had been canceled due to the pandemic. I was happy I was able to dial in and contribute, being so far away. I was also happy to see my friend Kapil's IT company, Streams Solutions (based in Ashburn, Virginia) expand by establishing an offshore delivery center near Delhi. I was glad to volunteer my time to be an advisory board member, giving Kapil and the company business advice as they expanded. I was proud of my friend for taking the plunge in starting his own company after years of working for others.

The Queen of Jugaad came through for me once again. My mom took a couple of my regular T-shirts, cut off their sleeves, and converted them to tank tops, like the kind they use in gyms. It did the job: they were easy to wear and comfortable in the hot weather.

Then it was my birthday. I was celebrating in India for the first time since I left the country thirty years earlier. The day started with heavy monsoon showers, just like it used to when I was young. I took my mom's blessings first thing in the morning and was delighted to speak to Jai and Arjun when they called. Family and friends from around the world also wished me well. I am truly blessed to be surrounded by some wonderful people. Sunita came over with Dhananjay and cooked my favorite chicken curry and custard. My mom made *gajar halwa* (carrot dessert pudding), and it was all delicious! Sunita also ordered a wonderful chocolate cake. We had a nice little family birthday celebration—of course enabled by social distancing!

I finally got a haircut at home after 110 days, a record

for me. The barber came to the apartment fully decked with PPE equipment. Although I felt like I was in an ICU, I was glad I got it done. I felt like a new person. I thought to myself, "This is absolutely a new normal."

Our anxiety peaked again as a family of four in my mom's building got infected with COVID-19. The pandemic had struck much closer to home now. The authorities sealed the floor, and we took some extra precautions, as both my mom and I were in the high-risk category. Around the same time, I had a severe case of Delhi belly, just as I had at Nimba in 2017. I also had some associated chills. We panicked, as these are two of the symptoms of the coronavirus infection. But luckily, like before, it turned out to be old-fashioned diarrhea. The chills didn't last long, and I had no fever or cough. Thank God!

I had another scare. Because of my dizziness, one morning I lost my balance, and to avoid a fall, I put pressure on my right arm to stabilize myself. Subsequently, my arm and shoulder started to hurt. Rupali told me to stop all the rehab exercises and to apply ice frequently. I was scared that I may have damaged the repaired tendons, and all the hard work over the last few months would go to waste. I went to Sportsmed. Dr. Ahuja did an ultrasound. Luckily, the repaired rotator cuff and the bicep were not damaged. The pain was from an aggravated trapezius, the muscle that extends at the back of the neck and shoulders. I was using more of this muscle now. Dr. Bhatia examined me, said everything was fine, and asked me to resume my therapy sessions.

I also noticed that it had been a full year since my

headaches had first spiked around the Fourth of July. In fact, the headaches were more than they were then. Although very frustrating, like before, I reminded myself that "it is what it is."

The pandemic continued to create havoc back home with increased number of cases and deaths. In India, too, cases were rising. Jai and I had an honest discussion about my not taking risks by coming back later in the summer under these conditions. Also, it did not make sense to go back in the winter, since they were expecting a second wave. Although things were not that great here, at least I had some help with my mom and sister. I was continuing to work on *One Fine Day* remotely and could continue to do so. So I made the major decision to further delay going back home. It would now probably be March or April of next year when I could hopefully return. I had no choice but to make this decision. I was now looking at eight more months in India. I had never stayed this long in the last thirty years, but it had to be done. My mom, sister, and Jai were relieved to hear that I extended my stay. Many friends agreed and supported my decision. I hoped and prayed the situation would be better by March or April. I was glad that I would still be able to vote in November, using absentee ballot. I terminated my Avalon lease early, as I was not returning until next year. It was nice of Susan to coordinate with the movers and the storage facility. Although I was saving money, I felt sad to leave Avalon. It was my first home in my new normal for the last year and half. I was also going to miss the friendly staff and residents. But I was not going to miss the complex's false fire alarms, which annoyed me and many other residents. Who knows if when I go back in the spring I will buy my own place or rent again at Avalon.

Unfortunately, my arm started to hurt again. It had nothing to do with my resumed tele-rehab sessions with Rupali. I overextended my arm while picking up a tissue paper from a box on the table. However, this time the pain was at the spot where the surgeries had been done—besides the continuing pain in the trapezius muscle. I stopped exercises again for a few days, iced the area, and prayed and hoped again that it was not serious. It was definitely frustrating and scary. My "it is what it is" mantra was being severely tested. Since the pain continued for a few days, I contacted Dr. Bhatia. He advised me to continue icing it and see how it felt a few days later. I guess I shouldn't take my new normal for granted.

The Real America

As I had postponed my plans to return home, I considered also delaying the publication of *One Fine Day*. But the more I thought about it, the more I realized that it was important to get it out sooner rather than later. It seemed to me that the entire world had its one fine day, indeed, and was facing a new normal due to the pandemic.

Not just back home, but many countries around the world were also facing protests against racial injustice. I felt that my messages of accepting life's changes no matter what they are and embracing the resulting new normal with positivity, grace, and gratitude should be heard. There is still tremendous good in the people of this world, regardless of their ethnicity, nationality, residential status, or economic stratum, and my story exemplifies this. *One Fine Day* could help people—especially now.

I have witnessed and experienced diversity in India. We also have it back in the States. People are from all walks of life and backgrounds. Over my last thirty years in the United States, I have never noticed or cared where a person is from or what religion, ethnicity, or color they might be. They are all fellow Americans to me. And most people are like me, whether they were born in that country or came from somewhere else. I bet it is true in many other places also. I am truly blessed to have experienced diversity both in my country of birth and in my adopted country. So I decided to keep the original launch schedule—early fall. Even though I was thousands of miles away, I could do all the launch tasks remotely.

I firmly believe, and I have seen this again and again, that for every one of the haters and racists out there, no matter where you are, there are many who are not. It is best to ignore those who spread hate and bigotry, but we shouldn't take what they do lying down. Demonstrate and make yourself heard, but do so peacefully. As the late John Lewis said, "When you see something that is not right, not fair, not just, you have to speak up. You have to say something; you have to do something."

Nothing justifies violence. Nothing. Nonviolence is the

only way to achieve justice. No matter what others might say, I have experienced the United States as a true melting pot. To me, that is the real America.

I was blessed to have been born in the land of Mahatma Gandhi and to have spent the last thirty years in the land of Martin Luther King, Jr. They both have shown the world what nonviolent civil disobedience can do. Whether it was Gandhi's Salt March for Indian independence from the British in 1930, King's March on Washington for equal rights in 1963, Rosa Parks's Montgomery Bus Boycott against segregation in 1955, or the suffrage parade for women's rights in 1913, peaceful protests have brought lasting social and political change. I am not naive enough to say that racism and discrimination aren't still problems. They absolutely are and can be found worldwide and exist not just within different communities but also within the same communities. Haters and bigots are within all communities. There are no exceptions. Still, we all should remember that there are generally more good people than haters and racists in every community or country. Nobody has a lock on being pious. I agree with the spiritual guru Deepak Chopra when he says, "Everybody has some divinity in them." No country on earth is perfect. Mahatma Gandhi says, "No culture can live if it attempts to be exclusive." We all have to remember that. We have to fight racial injustice in the world. No matter what our current challenges are with racism and discrimination, as an immigrant and a minority, I can say for the most part, America has lived up to its ideals of liberty, equality, justice, and fairness for all. Yes, we are not perfect, but we are definitely trying hard. I look at this from the standpoint not just of being a part of a minority group in the States, but also of being part of a majority in India.

My experiences in the States over the past thirty years have been overwhelmingly positive. Most of the United States is full of honest, generous, and kind people, no matter what their color or religion might be or whether or not they were born there. Even though I was ethnically and culturally different from many people in the States, I have been welcomed with open arms. I have been genuinely stunned at how accepting Americans are.

Life Goes On

As hard as the last few years have been—especially not working—to maintain my sanity, I looked at them as taking a sabbatical from work. Not that I was in any state to go back to work over the last three and a half years, but it has been definitely hard not to work for so long after working nonstop for twenty-four years. Whatever happened, I promised myself I would finish writing *One Fine Day* over the summer. Telling my story was a way of being productive and giving something back to the world. Besides helping others, writing *One Fine Day* is perhaps the first step toward reentering the working world. I might pursue writing and speaking as a new career or go back to my old one on a part-time basis—maybe do both. Only time will tell.

For the last three and a half years, I kept saying, "I feel

like I am intoxicated without alcohol." Once I slowly accepted my new normal, I now say, "I am intoxicated with life."

The only way for me to go on every day and be strong is to remind myself that, three and a half years ago, I was close to death. God decided it was not yet my time to leave this beautiful planet of ours, so I survived. I keep telling myself there has to be a reason I was saved; there has to be a reason for this second lease on life. Only God knows. My loved ones and I can only speculate. Maybe God wanted me to see Jai graduate and Arjun enter high school, or to write *One Fine Day* to help others going through life changes or adversity. Whatever the reason may be, I intend to live life fully with this second lease, no matter how difficult it is to face my new normal. I had to humor myself to keep myself sane. I have updated BS and AS to mean before stroke and after stroke.

Like everyone, I have dreams for the future. I am hoping and praying that one fine day I can:

- finish writing and launching *One Fine Day* by early fall

- return home in March or April of next year

- celebrate Jai's twenty-first birthday by having his first official alcoholic drink with his old man (after almost three and a half years of being dry— except that one Stella)

- see the world emerge from this pandemic crisis and from race issues, especially back home

- go back to work, any work, full- or part-time, old career or a new one
- translate *One Fine Day* into multiple languages, especially in my mother tongue, Marathi, and Hindi
- start driving again (Jai and I have agreed that he will take me to the same middle school parking lot where I taught him to drive)
- drive Arjun to the Washington Auto Show in downtown DC
- check out Jai's college campus as I have not been able to see it so far due to my health situation
- celebrate Jai's college graduation
- celebrate Arjun graduating from middle school and starting high school
- visit Nimba again, primarily to thank and express my gratitude to the amazing kind and generous staff there
- see Sikander find his dream job
- win in extra innings, whatever inning that may be;
- find that magic pill
- go on a fun vacation with the boys to a place they really want to go
- do some of the boys' favorite physical activities, like playing racquetball with Jai and Frisbee with Arjun

- visit Spain again with Los Cuotes
- take care of my mom in her golden years instead of her taking care of me
- resume my stalled workouts and rehab
- go to a Washington Nationals baseball game and resume our annual ritual of going to a football game of the Washington Football Team (their temporary new name, soon to have a permanent one) with Jai
- celebrate a Super Bowl win by the Washington Football Team. (I used to joke with Jai that they will win it all by the time he'd go to college. Now he will be graduating in a year and they are still nowhere close to going to the Super Bowl. It is now my new hope they will win it all before Arjun goes to college.)

• • •

"Storms don't last forever. Be patient and focus on the positive on the other side."

—CHRISTOPHER HUMMEL

Health Recovery Level:

Going for the remaining 60 percent.

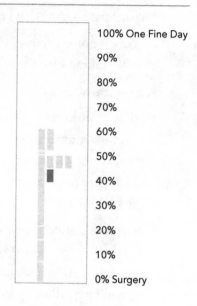

100% One Fine Day

90%

80%

70%

60%

50%

40%

30%

20%

10%

0% Surgery

SAMEERISM • Never give up no matter what you are going through. Hope for the best, but plan for the worst—always.

Epilogue

"How long should you try? Until."

JIM ROHN

If someone would have told me that I would have a life-altering stroke, still be rehabbing after three and a half years, be on long-term disability, not working, divorced, and writing a memoir, I would have laughed. But this is how life is. After facing these various life changes and adversities, I can see some silver linings in Sameer 2.0. I am much calmer and more patient than I was before. I have become more compassionate and empathetic and have a greater sense of gratitude. I am reinventing myself as a writer. Some aspects of the old me haven't changed. For one thing, I haven't lost my ability to laugh at life. I find that injecting humor into whatever I am experiencing is cathartic, like writing this book or keeping a daily journal. Finding a way to smile at what life has brought me has truly been a blessing.

My ongoing journey toward healing has taught me many things. I've learned to play the hand I was dealt, not the hand I wanted or thought I deserved. I've learned to accept my ever-changing new normal. I totally believe in the familiar expression, "When life gives you lemons, make lemonade." While it's natural to feel sorry for yourself after experiencing misfortune, playing the victim is not the answer. Coming to terms with my situation meant I had to accept some schadenfreude in folks I'd never expected would have such a reaction. Learning to not take things personally was a key part of my personal growth, so was gaining the ability to avoid comparing myself with others. Everyone has their own struggles and problems. If I was going to heal, it would be at my own pace, and that was perfectly okay. I've learned to approach healing with an open mind. My overall philosophy has been to consider different remedies and therapies from diverse medical traditions—old and new. I continue to say to my health care providers, "If it is not going to kill me, let's try it." I've balanced independence in my recovery with accepting help from others. Technology has played a critical role in making my life easier: speech recognition software, Skype or WhatsApp (for remote guided meditation sessions), WhatsApp messaging, larger text fonts on the computer screen, and more. With all the options available, I've learned how important it is to take ownership of your decisions, whether about medical treatments or other choices in life. I've received many ideas and suggestions from people who've meant well, but ultimately, I have had to decide for myself what route I've wanted to pursue. I have fully realized to surrender in the moment and not fight it.

Perhaps most importantly, I've learned that this journey is about more than just myself. Since my stroke, I've had my belief in the global village reaffirmed time and again. I could not help but notice that my caregivers back home were from all over the world and of different ethnicities. My neurosurgeon was Indian American; my ICU doctor was from Slovenia; my rehab doctor was a local Caucasian; my internist was from Thailand; my neurologists included an Indian, an African American, and an Iranian; and my physiatrist was Latino.

Many visitors who also came from diverse backgrounds stopped by to see me at Inova Fairfax and Mount Vernon Hospitals or at home or sent me good wishes via emails or phone: like Kedar and Vrinda's close friend Ashwin from New Jersey, who I knew well. It was great to see his smiling face. It was also great to see Anil's good friend Raj from Boston, even though I had never met him before. He knew Anil and I were close. My boss, Dave Boland, along with Joe Tria from Grant Thornton, who Monica and I knew; my Grant Thornton's Alexandria office colleagues Lisa, Mary, and Vishal, who with his wife brought me my favorite Dunkin' Donuts coffee. My ex-colleagues from 3Pillar Global, Ricky de Marchi Trevisan and Andy Zipfel, brought me some cookies to cheer me up. Monica's friend Amy Riolo got us dinner one evening, and Dr. Kanchan, a physician at Inova Fairfax Hospital, saw me a couple of times at the therapy center and gave us comfort. Dr. Naresh Khanna, Vrinda's cousin in Baltimore, dropped everything and came to see me in the ICU. My team at Grant Thornton (in the States and India) and my former coworkers at 3Pillar Global sent get-well videos that really lifted my spirits. Heather, Dave's wife, who Monica and I had never met, was in constant touch with Monica. The visits and well-wishes let me know I wasn't forgotten. They gave us moral support. "This is our real America. This is us." I thought.

I've also been truly blessed to have had so many people, irrespective of caste or religion, back in India helping me. At Nimba, many came from different Indian regions, which have unique cultures, traditions and, in many cases, different languages. There are twenty-two languages recognized in India's constitution. Masseurs Anoop, Prajeet, Sanil, from the southern state of Kerala; Kanta from Manipur; Chirag and Subhash from the western state of Gujarat; Amitabh from the northern state of Uttarakhand; Dr. Shyam from the southern state of Karnataka; Doctors Deepti, Benedict, and Arun from the southern state of Kerala; General Manager Mr. Saniyal and Nitin, front office manager from Uttar Pradesh; Sagar, the yoga teacher from the eastern state of Odisha; Deven, the dining room server from the northern state of Jammu and Kashmir; the local staff from the western state of Gujarat; receptionist, Hetal; gym and therapy center assistant, Hitesh; Doctors Saurabh and Himanshi at the therapy center; accountant, Harshadbhai; golf cart driver, Lal Bhai; and Ketul in the front office. Guests like my golf cart partner Amrita from the state of Gujarat; Dr. Meenakshi, whom I used to tease about her taste for *rajma chawal*, a popular vegetarian dish from her native Delhi; and Poonam from the western state of Rajasthan; Varsha and Amita, originally from Gujarat, who had moved to London; Azizbhai, a Bahraini; Taranpal Singh, Ashokbhai, Hansaben, and Mohammed from the UK; Mayur from the western state of Maharashtra, where I am from, who spoke to me in my mother tongue, Marathi, and respectfully called me *Dada*; Jess from Kenya; Terri from the States; Sandy and his wife from Mumbai; Alifia from Dubai; Poojal from Chennai; Rushabh from Gujarat; and an elderly lady also from Gujarat, whom we all called *Ba*, meaning "grandmother," in Gujarati. Ba reminded me of my late grandmother, to whom this book is dedicated, independent and feisty. In Mumbai, Anil's loving parents whom I'd known for many years; Sunita's good friend Fatema, who lived upstairs; several of my old friends like Neeta, Sharad, Rahul, Sharmila, and husband and wife Amod and Aparna when they visited Mumbai from Abu Dhabi. Their son Shantanu was getting ready to travel to the States for his master's degree program, and I was happy to share with him some words of wisdom and my experiences of coming to the States as a student twenty-eight years earlier. Vrinda's dad, Mr. Madhok (he is my father's age, but we are more like friends, as I am with his daughter), and her sister Archana and brother-in-law Dinesh; phone chats with my ex-colleague Balaji at Grant Thornton in Bangalore (Bengaluru, now) and my friend Maya.

My healing has been enhanced by old and new friends from around the world. There's a larger story in how people can work across borders and in cooperation with one another. I've been blessed to see this happen in my own life. I recently read something written in Sanskrit from ancient times: *Vasudhaiva kutumbka* ("The world is a family.") How absolutely true!

Like Sameer 2.0, I've also seen silver linings appear in the crises affecting the world around me. The global coronavirus pandemic led to reduced pollution levels, families spending more time together, and an increased awareness of the importance of better hygiene. People have rediscovered their sense of community, not just within families but also among friends and colleagues. Technologies like audio and video conferencing have given us new and creative ways to connect, communicate, and collaborate. The recent events in Minneapolis have increased the awareness of ugly racism, not just in the States but worldwide, and there is a general feeling and call for action to do something about this issue. Now it is up to each one of us to sustain these gains for as many people as possible. We are all in this together.

The rest of my story has yet to be written. No matter what happens, I will be grateful and enjoy and cherish every moment. Who knows where life will take me? I don't have the same goals or priorities as I had before my stroke. I am not saying that having specific goals or priorities is necessarily bad. All I want to say is that these life changes have made me realize that obsessing over them or being attached to them does not help. I do have a new mission in life: to help others. New goals and priorities will follow naturally. I firmly believe that if your sense of mission is strong, nothing will stand in your way. Nothing.

I've come to see that searching for a magic pill or potion—whether through Western or Eastern medicine—is not the answer. Physical rehab, spiritual care, and sheer grit is the only way to move forward. As I've said throughout this book, "it is what it is," and that means taking my new normal on its own terms, with acceptance but also with hope.

Every day I remind myself to count my blessings. They can be found even when the challenges seem steepest. Seeing how much I am surrounded by love and friendship has been one of the great rewards of this experience. In that sense, my one fine day—the very best kind—is already here.

• • •

"Accept the challenges of life and you'll continue to find that winning is the spirit of living . . . it's merely a state of mind."

—MYCHAL WYNN

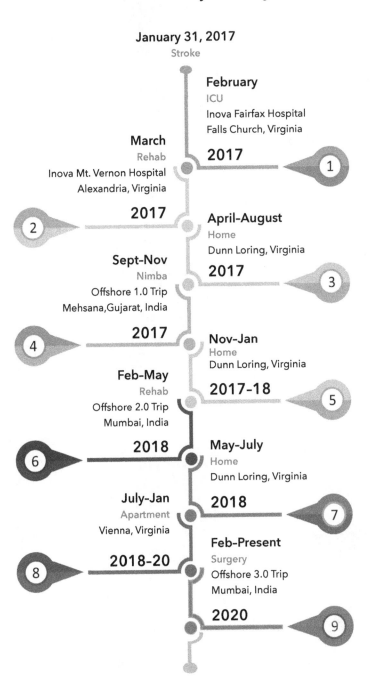

Timeline of My Journey

January 31, 2017
Stroke

February
ICU
Inova Fairfax Hospital
Falls Church, Virginia
2017   1

March
Rehab
Inova Mt. Vernon Hospital
Alexandria, Virginia
2017   2

April-August
Home
Dunn Loring, Virginia
2017   3

Sept-Nov
Nimba
Offshore 1.0 Trip
Mehsana,Gujarat, India
2017   4

Nov-Jan
Home
Dunn Loring, Virginia
2017-18   5

Feb-May
Rehab
Offshore 2.0 Trip
Mumbai, India
2018   6

May-July
Home
Dunn Loring, Virginia
2018   7

July-Jan
Apartment
Vienna, Virginia
2018-20   8

Feb-Present
Surgery
Offshore 3.0 Trip
Mumbai, India
2020   9

APPENDIX A

Holistic Providers around the World

There are many providers around the world that offer similar services to those at Nimba—from budget friendly to luxury. While I have not experienced these, I am aware of some of them.

Asia

- Amanbagh, Ajabgarh, Rajasthan, India
- Amanoi, Ninh Thuan, Vietnam
- Ananda in the Himalayas, Garhwal, Uttarakhand, India
- Anantara Peace Haven Tangalle Resort, Tangalle, Sri Lanka
- Atmaneem Nature Cure, Rajkot, Gujarat, India

- Atmantan Wellness Resort, Mulshi-Pune, Maharashtra, India
- Bamboo Yoga Retreat, Patnem, Goa, India
- Como Shambhala Estate, Bali, Indonesia
- Jindal Naturecure Institute, Bangalore, Karnataka, India
- Kairali–The Ayurvedic Healing Village, Palakkad, Kerala, India
- Kayakalp, Palampur, Himachal Pradesh, India
- Maya Spa, Kumarakom, Kerala, India
- Museflower Retreat and Spa, Chiang Rai, Thailand
- Soukya, Bangalore, Karnataka, India
- The Banjaran Hotsprings Retreat, Ipoh, Malaysia
- The Beach House, Goa, India
- The Yoga Barn, Bali, Indonesia
- Zen Resort, Bali, Indonesia

Europe

- Ayurveda Parkschlösschen, Traben-Trarbach, Germany
- European Ayurveda Resort Sonnhof, Tyrol, Austria
- Shanti-Som Wellbeing Being Retreat, Malaga, Spain
- Suncokret Body & Soul Retreat, Hvar Island, Croatia

- The Cover Mill, Worcestershire, United Kingdom
- Tapovan, Normandy, France

North America

- Grail Springs Retreat for Wellbeing, Bancroft, Ontario, Canada
- YO1 Health Resort, Monticello, New York, United States
- The Raj, Fairfield, Iowa, United States
- Villa Ananda, Near Puerto Vallarta, Mexico

South America

- Earthship Patagonia, Patagonia, Argentina
- La Casa de Loto, Guatapé, Antioquia, Colombia
- Willka T'ika, Cusco, Peru

Australia and New Zealand

- Bay of Islands Health Retreat, Kerikeri, New Zealand
- Samadhi, Daylesford, Victoria, Australia

Middle East and Africa

- Al Baleed Resort Salalah by Anantara, Oman
- Kamala Retreat House, Barrydale, South Africa
- Om Yoga, Marrakesh, Morocco

APPENDIX B

My Holistic
Treatments at Nimba

(Source: Dr. Shyam)

Abhyangam—Abhyanga ("oil massage") is a form of Ayurveda Panchakarma therapy that involves massage of the body with dosha-specific, warm, herb-infused oil. Ayurveda Panchakarma therapies are commonly pre-mixed with herbs for specific conditions. The name Panchakarma means "five actions," which is well-suited given the fact that this technique relies upon five distinctive basic activities that control the body, namely *vamanam* (vomiting), *virechanam* (purgation), *niruham* (colon enema), *Anuvaasan* (oil enema), and *nasyam* (inhalation of medicated oils). In other words, Panchakarma healing technique is a pillar on which a majority of Ayurvedic techniques stand.

Acupuncture—This involves the insertion of thin needles through your skin at strategic points on your body. A key component of traditional Chinese medicine, acupuncture is most commonly used to treat pain. Increasingly, it is being used for overall wellness, including stress management.

Antioxidant Therapy—Antioxidants are substances that may protect your cells against free radicals, which may play a role in heart disease, cancer, and other diseases. Free radicals are molecules produced when your body breaks down food or when you're exposed to tobacco smoke or radiation.

Choorna Pinda Swedanam—A similar procedure to patra pinda swedanam, powders of various herbs are used based on body type and health.

Deep Tissue Massage—This is a massage technique that's mainly used to treat musculoskeletal issues, such as strains and sports injuries. It involves applying sustained pressure, using slow, deep strokes to target the inner layers of your muscles and connective tissues. This helps to break up scar tissue that forms following an injury, and reduce tension in muscle and tissue.

Energy Healing—This is a traditional healing system that restores the balance and flow of energy throughout the body, mind, and soul. This technique works directly with the physical, emotional, and spiritual aspects of well-being. It is used to treat various medical conditions, especially ailments related to mental health. It addresses the illness caused due to disturbance of the energy flow in the body.

It is believed that when the energy flow gets fixed, the person is automatically cured.

Full Wet Sheet Pack—A procedure in which the patient is wrapped in a wet sheet outside of which are dry blanket coverings to regulate evaporation and to control the temperature.

Full-Body Mud Application—Mud is one of the five elements of nature that have immense effect on the body in health and sickness. The mud used for therapy is able to transfer heat, relaxing muscle tension, reducing pain and inflammation, improving circulation, and easing stiffness in joints. Due to its high mineral content, mud has a drawing effect on toxins and helps in detoxifying and healing.

Hydra Walk—Walking over pebbles in warm and cold water alternatively to alleviate any pain and build strength.

Jambeera Pinda Swedanam—Performed with the bolus of jambeera fruit pieces. It is usually done to help frozen shoulder, plantar fasciitis, and traumatic conditions.

Lomi Lomi Massage—This massage is one part of traditional native Hawaiian medicine that uses a combination of massage techniques, nut oils, and sometimes elements of prayer, breathing, and dance to restore energy and soothe the body. It is also known as the loving hands massage. This name helps to explain its principles: the massage works gently yet deeply into the muscles with continuous, flowing strokes, allowing the recipient to relax and give in to the nurturing touch.

Marma Massage–Marma points are energy points in the body used for healing in Ayurveda. They can be compared to acupuncture points in Chinese medicine. The focus of marma point massage is primarily to manipulate subtle energy, or prana, but physically they're also effective for relieving stiff muscles and boosting circulation.

Nasya Karma–Medicated drugs are administered through the nasal route to treat any problems related to sinus and upper respiratory tract.

Netra Vasti–Bathing the eyes with medicated clarified butter. Cleans the dust, dirt, and other substances that get trapped in the eyes.

Neutral Spinal Spray–This bath provides a soothing effect to the spinal column, thereby influencing the central nervous system. It is performed in a tub designed with its back raised to provide proper support to the patient's head. Spinal baths can be given in cold, neutral, and hot temperatures, or with hot and cold compresses on a localized area. Ice (cold compress) is the recommended treatment for acute injuries. It is especially helpful for reducing swelling and controlling pain. Ice is most effective when it is applied early and often for the first forty-eight hours. Heat (hot compress), on the other hand, increases circulation and raises skin temperature.

Njavarakizhi–A procedure by which the whole body or any specific part thereof is made to perspire by the application of certain medicinal drugs with *njavara*, a special variety of rice that grows in sixty days.

Nutrition and Diet Therapy (such as Alkaline Diet and Herbal Nutritional Juice)–According to this therapy, food must be taken in natural form. Fresh seasonal fruits, fresh greens, leafy vegetables, and sprouts are excellent for health.

Patra Pinda Swedanam–In this massage, leaves of medicinal plants along with other conventional drugs are roasted in a pan with a little oil, and a bolus is prepared by tying it in a cloth.

Physiotherapy and Occupational Therapy–Physiotherapy is treatment to restore, maintain, and make the most of a patient's mobility, function, and well-being. Occupational therapy is used to treat injured, ill, or disabled people through the therapeutic use of everyday activities. It helps to develop, recover, improve, and maintain the skills needed for daily living and working.

Pizhichil—This involves the squeezing of warm medicated oil onto the body of the patient from a piece of cloth that is periodically soaked in a vessel containing the oil. *Pizhichil* means "squeezing."

Psychological Counseling—This can help people with physical and emotional health issues, improve their sense of well-being, alleviate feelings of distress, and resolve crises.

Reflex Massage—Reflexology is the application of appropriate pressure to specific points and areas on feet, hands, ears, and other body parts. This healing practice is based on the principle that there are reflex points on the feet that correspond to the body's different organs and glands. Reflexology is more than just a foot massage, as its therapeutic effects are vast and help to achieve balance.

Shiro Vasti—Herbal oil head bath therapy is an Ayurvedic therapy that focuses on the "roof of the human body." The medicated oil, warmed to body temperature, is poured into a cap and allowed to soak into the scalp until the manifestation of proper signs of efficient treatment. Psychosomatic diseases, depression, chronic headaches, migraines, insomnia, and many other conditions are successfully treated in Ayurveda by shiro vasti.

Shirodhara—The therapeutic administration of warm oils to the center of the forehead in a continuous stream. Designed to eliminate toxins and mental exhaustion as well as relieve stress and any ill effects.

Swedana Karma—Meaning "fomentation," a thermal or non-thermal procedure that cures stiffness, heaviness, and cold, and produces sweating in the body.

Swedish Massage—Massage that uses light to moderate pressure. It relieves knots and tension that we often experience in our neck, shoulders, and back. Also helps to relieve headaches caused from tension.

Udvartanam—One of the most sought-after Ayurvedic treatments for weight loss. It is a unique deep tissue massage that uses herbal powders and oils.

Yoga Therapy—This is the application of yoga practices to alleviate physical and mental health conditions with the view of promoting self-care and encouraging overall well-being. While the practice of yoga in general aims to cultivate the body and mind, and hence has the potential for therapeutic effects, yoga therapy uses specific practices and their known benefits to help alleviate or heal mental and physical ailments.

APPENDIX C

Newer Treatments in Western Medicine

I have tried some of these following treatments.

Biofeedback—This is a therapy technique used to treat conditions like migraines, chronic pain, and others. Neurofeedback is a type of biofeedback used to treat some brain disorders.

Botox—Besides cosmetic benefits, Botox is also used for treating chronic migraine headaches.

CBD Oils—Cannabidiol (CBD) is an extract from the cannabis plant. The tetrahydrocannabinol (THC) is the main compound found in cannabis and causes the sensation of getting high. But CBD does not do that. It can help alleviate pain and anxiety. It is approved by the FDA for treatment of epilepsy in children. Other benefits may include treating neurological disorders, diabetes, heart issues, and certain kinds of cancer. However, more research and evidence are needed to fully understand the benefits of CBD.

Wholetones–Music has a universal language and, since ancient times, has been used to heal. For me, it unites people by knocking down the walls that separate us. Wholetones (www.wholetones.com) is frequency-based healing music therapy used to reduce anxiety, help you sleep, and fight diseases.

APPENDIX D

Yoga
Exercises

(Source: Dr. Shyam)

There are many yoga exercises for general wellness and well-being. Here are some I continue to do. You may hear from different people about how long to do exercises and how much you should do. Being a practical person, I believe you should do as much as you can and not worry about how much others say you should do. There are many tutorials online and teachers who can teach you the proper techniques. The best part is that these exercises don't cost you anything. You don't have to get a gym membership or buy training equipment, and you can do them in the privacy and comfort of your home.

Bhramari Pranayama—The original word in the term is *bhramar* ("humming bee"). This pranayam relates to the word "bhramar," that is the sound that bhramar emits. The characteristics of this pranayama is to create a sound like that of a humming bee while performing inhalation or exhalation. You close your ears with two fingers and then make this sound.

> SAMEERISM • I try to do this after my fifteen minutes of meditation in the morning. I do about ten repetitions, ten to twelve seconds each.

Meditation—Meditation is a state of pure consciousness and is the art of concentration. When you meditate, you focus your attention on an object or a thought or an activity, like music or your breath, thus bringing you mental calm and peace.

> SAMEERISM • How long to meditate is the big question on many folks' minds. I try to do it for fifteen minutes in the morning and fifteen minutes in the evening. When I meditate, I do guided meditation, whether remotely with Sagar, with one of the many YouTube videos offering guided meditation, or with music. (It can be any music: classical, instrumental, Eastern or Western, or other relaxing types of music, just not rock, pop, or rap.) Also, there are many apps and sites which offer guided meditation. One I like is Headspace.
>
> Meditation is not easy. If other thoughts come into your mind (and they will), it's perfectly okay,

don't get mad. Let them come. But don't dwell on them, and focus your attention on your breathing.

Om Chanting—"Om" is the core mantra from which other mantras come from. The spelling is o-m, but the actual mantra consists of three letters a-u-m. You exhale the sound, and when you do, the vibrations it creates travel from lower abdomen, to upper abdomen, and to the head. You feel energized.

> SAMEERISM • I try to do this after my meditation and pranayam. I do the a-u-m chant about three to five times, ten to twelve seconds each.

Pranayam—Pranayam provides a vital bridge between the body and the mind. By controlling the breath, you can control the mind. When a person is angry or agitated, their breath is fast, disturbed, and shallow.

> SAMEERISM • I close one nostril and then inhale and exhale from the other one. Then I do the same with the other nostril. I do five repetitions for each nostril. For me, it is like doing a cardio workout.

Shavasana—*Shava* means "corpse" and *asana* is "posture or body position." Thus, in shavasana we have to be as motionless and without activity, like a dead body. However, in shavasana we obviously are not dead; the witness consciousness remains alive. If practiced properly, we come out of shavasana completely fresh, invigorated, and relaxed.

> SAMEERISM • I try to do this when I go to bed. I do it for fifteen minutes in my bed, lying still and relaxing. I set an alarm before doing this, so I know when fifteen minutes are up. You may think it's easy to do this, but it's not. It's very challenging to lie motionless. Fifteen minutes in that state is an eternity. But at the end of it, like meditation, your body and mind calm down, and you sleep better.

Trataka—The practice of gazing steadily, without blinking, on a small object is known as *trataka*. It develops profound concentration, the ability to hold and fix our attention on an object as well as to make the object disappear.

> SAMEERISM • Whenever I do this, I light a candle and focus my attention on the tip and center of the flame for ten minutes or so, or until my eyes become watery as if I am crying, since I am not blinking. Along with concentration, it's also good for your eyes. I used to do this daily, but now do it whenever I can.

APPENDIX E

Service Providers

The following providers have assisted me greatly. If you have a need, give them a try. They are excellent, and all hardworking and diligent.

Care: India

- Nimba Nature Cure (Naturopathy and Wellness Retreat), www.nimba.in
- Sagar Agrawal (remote meditation sessions), yogahabhyasa@gmail.com
- Nagesh Dhage, Mumbai (masseur), cell number, 961-981-7465
- Anand Kasbe, Mumbai (home aide), cell number, 965-362-9312

- Rupali Kuckian, Mumbai (physical therapist), cell number, 932-027-9320
- Sportsmed, Mumbai (injury management), www.sportsmed.in

Care: USA

- Inova Fairfax Hospital, Falls Church, VA, and Mount Vernon Hospital, Alexandria, VA, rehab centers (www.inova.org/our-services /inova-rehabilitation-services)
- MedStar Georgetown University Hospital Headache Center, Washington, DC (www.medstargeorgetown.org/our-services /neurosciences/headache-center)
- Dr. Susan Ammerman, clinical psychologist, Fairfax, VA (www.psychologytoday.com/us /therapists/susan-k-ammerman-fairfax-va/280095)
- Ann Marie Barrie, Select Physical Therapy, Annandale, VA (www.selectphysicaltherapy.com)
- Alex Lovallis, Sheltering Arms, Richmond, VA (www.shelteringarms.com)
- Dr. Anthony Avery, Orthopedics, Ortho Virginia, Mclean, Virginia (www.orthovirginia.com)

Book Publishing

- Amy Hayes, book cover designer
  (www.amyhayes.co)
- kn literary arts, writing and editorial services
  (www.knliterary.com)
- Pub Site, author website platform
  (www.pub-site.com)
- Thierry Sagnier, writing and editorial services
  (www.sagnier.com)

Other

- Total Tech Geeks, in the DC area, computer
  repairs, data recovery (www.totaltechgeeks.com)
- Sam, barber (www.barberelite.com)

Further Reading

Books

Bernhard, Toni. *How to Be Sick: A Buddhist-Inspired Guide for the Chronically Ill and Their Caregivers*. Somerville, MA: Wisdom Publications, 2010.

Bernstein, Gabrielle. *The Universe Has Your Back: Transform Fear to Faith*. Carlsbad, CA: Hay House, 2016.

Chopra, Deepak. *The Seven Spiritual Laws of Success: A Practical Guide to the Fulfillment of Your Dreams*. Novato, CA: New World Library, 1994.

Dow, Mike and David Dow. *Healing the Broken Brain: Leading Experts Answer 100 Questions about Stroke Recovery*. Carlsbad, CA: Hay House, 2017.

Hay, Louise. *You Can Heal Your Life*. Carlsbad, CA: Hay House, 1984.

Kushner, Harold S. *When Bad Things Happen to Good People*.
    New York: Anchor Books, 1981.
Sandberg, Sheryl and Adam Grant. *Option B: Facing
    Adversity, Building Resilience, and Finding Joy*. New
    York: Alfred A. Knopf, 2017.

Articles

Janecic, Phil. "Best Motivational Article Ever."
    Mind of Steel. Accessed August 20, 2020.
    www.themindofsteel.com/best-motivation-ever.
Moret, Shaneé. "Humanity Is Not Canceled."
    March 19, 2020. www.medium.com/@shaneemoret
    /humanity-is-not-canceled-69a26baa5eee.
Thirumalai, Sanjay. "Hacking Happiness." LinkedIn.
    December 22, 2017. www.linkedin.com/pulse
    /hacking-happiness-sanjay-thirumalai.
———. "Happiness Amidst a Pandemic." Thrive Global.
    March 20 2020. www.thriveglobal.com/stories
    /happiness-amidst-a-pandemic.
Trip Trivia. "Where Did Yoga Come From?" December
    11, 2019. www.triptrivia.com/where-did-yoga-come
    -from/XphLiNfEsAAGy_XV.

Author Website

www.sameerbhide.com
- Photos: several photos from my journey
- Videos: links to many videos I have found that have touched my heart and inspired me
- Quotations: additional inspiring quotes

Acknowledgments

From the bottom of my heart I want to thank and sincerely express my gratitude to many of the hundreds of kind, generous, and compassionate caregivers, friends, family, colleagues, neighbors, and supporters here in my adopted country of thirty years and my country of birth who have helped me tremendously. My family and I are truly blessed to be surrounded by these extraordinary people—some of whom were total strangers—especially those who have helped us over the difficult last three and a half years of our lives. I could not help but notice these are people from all walks of life with very diverse backgrounds.

My friends include Anil and Aparna, in Boston; Kedar and Vrinda; Makarand and Meghana, in New Jersey; Kedar and Siddharth, in London; Mohan and Meera, in Mumbai; Lydia and Chandu, Susan, Ron and Britt, Kyran, Sal, Ana and

Luis, Brian and Valerie, Emanuele and Debbie, and Vinu and Aradhana, all in the DC area.

Besides our diverse friends, we are also fortunate to have had support from a caring family; my mom, my sister, Sunita, my brother-in-law Dhananjay, in Mumbai; my parents-in-law in Delhi; my sister-in-law Arti and brother-in-law Sumir, in Arizona; Monica's cousin Shelley and her husband, Rahul, in Virginia; and my aunt Dr. Smita and her family, in Maryland.

There are also so many other kind souls all over the world who I would also like to thank, who sent not just me but my family so much needed prayers, well-wishes, support, positive vibes, get-well cards, flowers, candy, and food. Many of them have been there for me in my ongoing recovery journey. Some are mentioned below. I apologize in advance if I may have forgotten or missed anyone. You can blame it on the loss of some brain cells due to the brain surgeries. Mike Lipka, Kapil and Sharon Sharma, Mr. and Mrs. Sudhakar, Ashok and Seema Dhoop, Harsh and Shirley Taur, Dr. Naresh Khanna, Raju Khanna, Sonali and Sudhir Seth, Nisha and KN Vinod, Madhu and Surfy Rehman, Roopa and Manish Wardekar, the Mehra family in Toronto, Kanta and Prem Saigal, Garima and Gaurav Saigal, Anu and Ankur Rohatgi, Saroj and Gulshan Khanna, Dr. Kanchan Anand, Kshama and Mahesh Kheny, Sundari and Ashwin Rao, Renuka Hegde-Sathe and Nikhil Sathe, Smita Sundd and Vikrant Saraswat, Geeta and Sriram Damaraju, Seema and Manoj Shahane, Deepa and Rahul Agarwal, Chitra and Sambasivsan Bhaskar, Amy Riolo, Ramin

Ganeshram, Aviva Goldfarb, Nevin Martell, Donna and Kevin Berk, Kathleen Flinn and Mike Klozar, Kathy and Hadi Alsegaf, Janet and Jim Walters, Marcia and Bill Tomson, Eman and Rami Safadi, Ajay and Vandana Taneja, Sonia and Jasmeet Anand, Ibtasim and Yahya Alshawkani, Bob and Nancy Winn, Sayli and Mike Moskowitz; many folks from Grant Thornton, Mike McGuire, Brad Preber, Sri Sastry, Dave Boland, Sanjay Thirumalai, Vishal Chawla, Doug Kalish, and many others; Heather Boland, David Dewolf, and many others from 3Pillar Global; Vernon Hollidge, Kevin Boyce, Beth Jacobs, Soichi Ishiguro, Michael Ekman, Asa Campbell, Sandy and Bob Turba, Jim Lee, Anil Purohit, Amod and Aparna Tilak, Dr. Anant Joshi, Vivek Joshi, Mr. and Mrs. M. G. Bhide, Mr. and Mrs. Junnarkar, Mrs. Barwe, Mrs. Thakur, Mr. and Mrs. Sawaikar, Mr. and Mrs. Phadnis, Mrs. Kulkarni, Gauri Mandke, Manjiri Shirole, Sushma and Shankar Khasnis, Niteen and Aditi Datar, Mugdha and Sanjay Asrani, Sharad Sharma, Neeta Nene, Ashutosh and Sharmila Bijoor; and Inova Fairfax Hopital's Patient and Family Advisory Committee (PFAC) members.

A very special thanks to the entire team at Fairfax Inova Hospital for saving my life, especially Dr. Nilesh Vyas, Dr. Svet Djurkovic, Stacia Singh, RN; my outpatient therapists Theresa Bell, Lisa Molofski, Lisa Nihil, and Bethany, and staff members Sheryl, Lauren, and others; the entire team at Inova Mount Vernon Rehab Hospital led by Dr. Gisolfi, for their help in getting me better; DC area doctors who are helping me heal further, especially Dr. Suneetha

Manem, Dr. Rachel Ngernmaneepothong, and Dr. Susan Ammerman; my therapists at Select Physical, Anne, Marie, Barry, and Alex Lovallis; and my doctors in India, Dr. Satish Khadilkar, Dr. Deepak Bhatia, and Dr. Shyam Nidugala.

I am also truly grateful and thankful for the many people who have inspired, guided, encouraged, provided honest feedback and input for *One Fine Day*. But the two friends I would really like to highlight who have really helped me shape my memoir are Brian in Virginia and Anil in Boston. A special thank-you to them! Also special thanks to Kelly Notaras, the founder of kn literary arts, and her outstanding team of Jamaica Stevens, Heidi Hudak, Annie Wylde, Jason Buchholz, and Alexandra Oliver for their help with *One Fine Day*. Also heartfelt thanks to my ghostwriter, Barry Alfonso, for helping me write it and for his patience with me. I have to say it was a great team effort between us. I would not have been able to do this without the help of Kelly and kn literary arts. And sincere thanks to Thierry Sagnier for his help with fine tuning my writing. And heartfelt thanks to Brad Preber for regularly keeping in touch and encouraging me, and writing a beautiful foreword for the book. Also, thanks to Hay House for offering their free master class and their online writer's workshop, which inspired me further to write *One Fine Day*.

About Sameer Bhide

Sameer underwent a left sub-occipital craniectomy and hematoma evacuation for a likely ruptured cerebral cavernous malformation (abnormality), which was the cause of his hemorrhagic stroke. It is genetic and extremely rare. According to the *Handbook of Neurosurgery* by Mark S. Greenberg, which Sameer's neurosurgeon refers to, this abnormality develops in about 3,300 to 58,800 people in the US. But when it results in a hemorrhage like Sameer's (rupturing of the abnormality), it is even rarer, accounting for only 86 to 1,730 people in the US per year. Many of those die. Sameer is extremely grateful for being in that survivor's group. However, not all these abnormalities result in a hemorrhage. Many people have the abnormality but nothing happens to them.

Although Sameer's MRIs and CAT scans are now normal, he still continues to struggle with dizziness, headaches, and instability in his balance. His doctors aren't sure if these symptoms will disappear completely. Sameer's vision, speech, and body strength, though, have improved greatly due to many aggressive therapies—physical, occupational, speech, vestibular, and vision in the United States, and in India, naturopathy and holistic treatments like acupuncture, energy healing, raga therapy (music), and various Ayurvedic treatments and practices such as yoga, meditation, vegetarian diet, and massages.

Despite the huge upheaval in his life, Sameer is very grateful and thankful for the many fortunate breaks he had after his stroke. Very quickly after his stroke, he was on his way to the ER, and within two hours, he was in surgery with a top neurosurgeon who specializes in cases like his.

Prior to his stroke, Sameer worked for almost twenty-four years in different roles in management, technology consulting, and knowledge management and sales at Ernst & Young, Kana, Ellucian, Wilmerhale LLP, Tata Consultancy Services (TCS), 3Pillar Global, and Grant Thornton LLP.

Sameer was born in Pune, India, and graduated with an accounting undergraduate degree in 1989 from the University of Mumbai. He then moved to the United States where, in 1991, he completed a bachelor's degree in management from the University of Lynchburg, Virginia, and in 1993, an MBA from Drake University in Des Moines, Iowa.

CPSIA information can be obtained
at www.ICGtesting.com
Printed in the USA
FSHW011738081220
76711FS

9 781735 693446